CW00430208

THE GARDENING YEAR

THE GARDENING YEAR

LANCE HATTATT

Illustrations by
ELAINE FRANKS

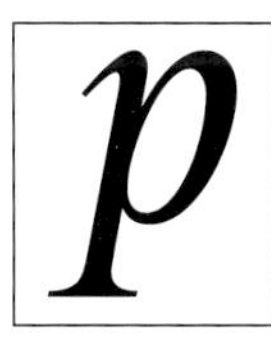

This is a Parragon Book
This edition published in 2003

Parragon
Queen Street House
4 Queen Street
Bath BA1 1HE, UK

Produced for Parragon by
Robert Ditchfield Publishers

ISBN 1-40540-435-3

A copy of the British Library Cataloguing in Publication Data is available from the Library.

Typeset by Action Publishing Technology Ltd, Gloucester
Colour origination by Colour Quest Graphic Services Ltd.
London E9
Printed and bound in China

Acknowledgements

Many of the photographs were taken in the author's garden, Arrow Cottage, Ledgemoor, Weobley. The publishers would also like to thank the many people and organizations who have allowed photographs to be taken for this book, including the following:

Mr and Mrs Terence Aggett; Barnsley House; Polly Bolton, Nordybank Nurseries, Clee St Margaret; Bromsberrow Place Nurseries, Ledbury; Lindsay Bousfield, Acton Beauchamp Roses, Worcester; Burford House, Tenbury Wells; Dr Lallie Cox, Woodpeckers, Marlcliff, Bidford-on-Avon; Kim Davies, Lingen; Dinmore Manor; Richard Edwards, Well Cottage, Blakemere; Haseley Court; The Hon Mrs Peter Healing, The Priory, Kemerton; Hergest Croft, Kington; Hidcote Manor Garden (National Trust); Kim Hurst, The Cottage Herbery, Boraston, Tenbury Wells; Mr and Mrs J James; Mrs David Lewis, Ash Farm, Much Birch; Mrs M T Lloyd, Edenbridge House, Edenbridge; Mr and Mrs Roger Norman; Mrs Richard Paice, Bourton House; The Picton Garden, Colwall; Powis Castle (National Trust); Royal Botanic Gardens, Kew; RHS Garden, Wisley; Sissinghurst Castle (National Trust); Stone House Cottage Gardens, Stone; Malley Terry; Raymond Treasure, Stockton Bury Farm, Kimbolton; Wakehurst Place (National Trust); Wyevale Garden Centre, Hereford; York Gate, Leeds.

The photograph of *Rosa* 'Royal William' on page 117 is reproduced by kind permission of Mattocks Roses and the photograph on page 148 by kind permission of Dr Lallie Cox.

THE AIM of this book is to show the gardener how to make the most of his or her garden through the months of the year. There are of course many factors that can affect plants and the work that has to be done at different times – climate, weather, soil and even a gardener's own timetable of planting and pruning. Plants will flower earlier in some areas, later elsewhere; blooms will be delayed in some years and hastened in others. But if allowance is made for such variables, this book will provide a helpful working schedule not only for the gardener who seeks to ensure that the garden is never bare of interest but also for the occasional gardener who wants to know what will happen and when.

Symbols

Where measurements are given, the first is the plant's height followed by its spread.
The following symbols are also used in this book:

- ❍ = thrives best or only in full sun
- ◐ = thrives best or only in part-shade
- ● = succeeds in full shade
- E = evergreen

Where no sun symbol and no reference to sun or shade is made in the text, it can be assumed that the plant tolerates sun or light shade.

Poisonous Plants

Many plants are poisonous and it must be assumed that no part of a plant should be eaten unless it is known that it is edible.

CONTENTS

THE GARDENING YEAR

THERE IS something pleasantly reassuring about the unhurried, cyclical pattern of the gardening year. With the gradual unfolding of each season the gardener experiences a deep sense of the harmony and continuity of nature. As the months turn, so familiar, new or previously unnoticed sights are revealed which constantly serve to raise the spirit, excite the eye and, importantly, renew resolve. Work in such moments may be set aside, forgotten altogether. What matters in these instances is not what has gone before but the pleasure of what lies ahead.

SPRING

Spring ushers in one of the busiest times in the garden. It is also one of the most satisfying. All the potential and promise of the whole year is captured in the first showing of early daffodils, scillas and tulips. Delicate cardamines, double primulas and showy ranunculus all contribute colour and life to borders which for too long have seemed bare. As the weeks pass the rock garden is alight with tiny, alpine treasures, massed bedding creates startling impact and wonderful spring trees and shrubs thrill with fine flowers.

Sowing of seed, whether of vegetables, herbs or annual flowers, begins in earnest as the soil warms under spring sunshine. At this time of the year weeds appear, apparently overnight, calling for vigilance and the regular wielding of hand fork or hoe; alternatively, mulching of beds or planting ground cover will help to maintain order. These are months for the division of perennials, for planning the pots and containers you will use in summer displays as well as routine tasks like staking, conditioning soil and lawn care. As flowering bulbs go over, dead heading will avoid untidiness. Where these have been established in grass, mowing should be delayed until foliage has completely died down.

Nurseries and garden centres hold their largest stocks in springtime. A visit will reward you with new and unusual plants to revitalize tired borders, to fill recently developed areas, or simply, to plug the gap between spring and summer. Planting provides a welcome opportunity to look carefully at combinations of colour, form and texture. Use spring days to eliminate acknowledged mistakes, to correct minor errors and to rearrange beds and borders in pursuit of that unreachable goal, perfection.

SUMMER

Summer is synonymous with scent and colour. Fragrant lilies, garden pinks, old fashioned stocks, tobacco plants and violas perfume the air from daybreak until dusk. Borders overflow with a tapestry of mid-season bulbs, herbaceous perennials and annuals, a controlled confusion so dear to a gardener's heart. Roses, the queen of all the summer shrubs, compete with clematis, honeysuckles, lavenders and mock oranges to fill the garden with a wealth of beauty. As the season progresses so the pastel hues of early summer deepen. Pale pinks, lemon yellows, lavenders and blues are replaced with fiery red, orange and gold, violet and indigo.

Enjoy summer meals, often taken

Opposite: China Pink tulips under a crab apple.

The ornamental onion *Allium aflatunense*.

outside, with produce freshly harvested from the kitchen garden. Sitting-out areas, transformed with seasonal bedding, invite moments of idleness and relaxation. Even the regular tasks of lawn mowing and edging, of watering pots, dead heading and of summer pruning all need to be carried out at a more leisurely pace during long, hot days. These are holiday months and days out are to be anticipated with pleasure. Plan to visit some of the many lovely gardens which are open to the public as a source of inspiration.

Autumn

Traditionally autumn prefaces the end of the year, anticipates the onset of winter. Not so in the garden where, amidst the obvious signs of decay, fresh life stirs and a period of feverish, but satisfying activity begins.

Border preparation comes into its own as

Delphiniums and *Rosa* 'Fantin-Latour'.

the days shorten. Whilst the spent stems of summer are cleared away and dying leaves are raked from under shrubs and hedges, the newly revealed earth waits, freshly forked, for life to recommence. Warm earth and autumnal rains encourage seasonal planting. Evergreen trees and shrubs moved into new positions now will put out fibrous roots before the year turns. Bulbs, legacies of summer lists, set out in open ground will, within a few short months, bring vitality to sleeping borders. September, October, or even November in milder areas, are the months in which to plant out spring bedding into final positions. Winter-flowering pansies, wallflowers, polyanthus and forget-me-nots, all easily raised from seed, will provide a wealth of colour in the weeks to come.

Work in the kitchen garden begins apace. With the main harvest over, vegetable beds are laid bare. Digging and

Autumnal dahlias and *Fuchsia magellanica* 'Alba'.

manuring ensures the ground is in fine fettle for the new season's crops. Seed sowing gets under way with carrots, cauliflower and lettuce for winter salads. Hardwood cuttings of currants, figs and gooseberries, taken as soon as leaves fall, should readily root in holding beds before the soil cools down.

Autumn planting, the propagation of garden shrubs, the gathering of seed and the making of crumbly leaf mould to enrich the borders at a later date, these are all activities which, for the expectant gardener, keep the wheels of the garden year in motion.

Hamamelis mollis, the fragrant Chinese witch hazel.

WINTER

The hours of daylight in winter are frustratingly short. Often the weather is bleak and inhospitable: fog, wind, rain, ice and snow all conspire to make outdoor work particularly uninviting. On such days the fireside beckons, for these are times for reflection, contemplation and planning. In looking back over the year's achievements and, as importantly, failures, salutory lessons may be learned. Taking stock of what has been, and what is, can prompt positive action. This is a time to consider the reshaping of beds and borders, the improvement of planting schemes, the repositioning of dominant features, the effective siting of pots – in short, a critical appraisal of the whole garden. On bright days, days borrowed from spring, a journey around the garden, armed with notebook and pencil, can be a most pleasurable and rewarding activity. Indoors, seed lists and the new season's catalogues are there to be pored over, favourite garden books and magazines reread and re-examined, and even summer outings to gardens planned.

With the onset of a new calendar year winter sunshine, still rationed, becomes a powerful, irresistible force. Outside, neglected ground can be satisfactorily cleared and dug, paths made or relaid, toolsheds tidied and exciting new projects undertaken. As the year advances routine pruning gets under way. Included at this time are fruit trees and bushes, late flowering shrubs, roses, and those clematis requiring to be hard pruned.

But the winter garden is not without interest and colour. Viburnums and hamamelis provide deliciously fragrant early blooms, skimmias and hollies are bright with berry, the stems of dogwoods and willows gleam in sunlight and the ground is carpeted with first flowers. Amongst these are sparkling cyclamen, winter aconites, snowdrops, stalwart crocus and lovely miniature iris. The year moves on, the days are warmer, spring is in the air.

JANUARY–FEBRUARY

FOR THE GARDENER these are exciting times. Days may be short and drear, light levels low, the nights long and cold but outside, even in this the bleakest of periods, the garden is far from lacking in interest.

Early bulbs push through the cold earth to lighten the dark days. Lovely dwarf iris, drifts of crocus, pale snowdrops with sword-like leaves, tiny daffodils, all are the welcome harbingers of approaching spring. Leaves, retained throughout the winter, are prominent now. Lustrous ivies, clinging to walls and trees, shiny hollies, glistening laurels, the dull copper of beech, each contributes form and pattern to a bare landscape. Trees, hedges and shrubs, already in bud, emphasize the framework of the garden.

Iris unguicularis One of the joys of winter. Rhizomes of the Algerian iris require an open, sunny position and sharp drainage. ○, E, 60 × 30cm/ 2 × 1ft

◆ *Named forms are worth seeking out. Of note are 'Mary Barnard' and 'Walter Butt'. 'Alba' has white falls marked yellow.*

Crocus tommasinianus This little crocus with its starry, lavender-purple coloured flowers is ideal for the rock garden. Once established it should seed freely. ◐, 10cm/4in

Bergenia purpurascens Enjoy the rich, ruby red of these bold leaves throughout the winter months. Later, as the weather warms, they will revert to green. E, 30 × 45cm/ 1 × 1½ft

Cyclamen coum Often seen offered for sale as flowering pot plants, these cyclamen are naturally woodlanders. To thrive, tubers should be planted in autumn in reasonably well-drained soil enriched with leaf mould or good garden compost in a position where they are unlikely to dry out in summer. 10 × 15cm/4 × 6in

◆ *Before planting soak in water, to which has been added systemic fungicide, for a period of twenty-four hours. This will encourage activation of dormant tubers.*

Galanthus nivalis Division of snowdrops should take place, 'in the green', immediately after flowering. Simply lift, carefully divide the bulbils and replant. ◐, ●, 15 × 15cm/6 × 6in

Eranthis hyemalis Bright yellow, cheery flowers make winter aconites particularly welcome. Plant the tubers in autumn in semi-shaded, humus-rich soil. ◐, 10 × 15cm/4 × 6in

Helleborus lividus Fine foliage and prettily shaded flowers. Less hardy than some hellebores, lividus should be placed in a sheltered position. E, ◐, 45 × 45cm/1½ × 1½ft

***Helleborus foetidus* 'Wester Flisk'** Brilliant red stems and grey-green leaves distinguish this form of hellebore from others. All hellebores enjoy an annual mulch of well rotted compost in the early part of the year before flowering. At the same time the appearance of the plant is greatly improved with the removal of old leaves. E, ◐, 45 × 45cm/1½ × 1½ft

◆ Helleborus orientalis *will cross with each other to produce seedlings in a wide range of colours. These vary from desirable near-black to magenta to deep yellow.*

***Iris reticulata* 'Harmony'** Sometimes reluctant to flower, reticulata irises should be planted in autumn to a depth of around 10cm/4in. ❍, 10 × 15cm/4 × 6in

Chionodoxa luciliae Glory of the Snow is the common name. Unfussy as to soil or situation, they should be left undisturbed to increase by self-sown seed. 10cm/4in

Crocus Spring-flowering crocuses appear to flourish when, as here, they are planted naturally in grass. Delay mowing until the flowers and foliage have died down. 10cm/4in

Narcissus bulbocodium Miniature daffodils, though seemingly quite frail, are in fact robust little bulbs which, planted deeply in well drained soil, will reappear year after year. Dead head but allow leaves to die down. ❍, 15 × 20cm/6 × 8in

◆ *Use small bulbs in pots for splashes of instant colour.* Narcissus cyclamineus *and* N. *'February Gold' both lend themselves to pot cultivation.*

INDOOR GARDENS

For those fortunate enough to own a heated greenhouse or, better still, a conservatory, it is possible to have something of interest, even exotic, in flower virtually at all times. Tender plants will perform well given sufficient heat and light. Shown here is the enticing passion flower, *Passiflora antioquiensis*, which can be maintained in bloom through the winter months.

Cymbidium Cymbidiums are epiphytic orchids. Several forms bloom in winter in a cool greenhouse. E, 75cm/30in

WINTER BARK

Once bare of leaves interesting and attractive tree trunks come into their own. Plant such a tree as the centrepiece of a winter garden or as an out-of-season highlight in the main borders.

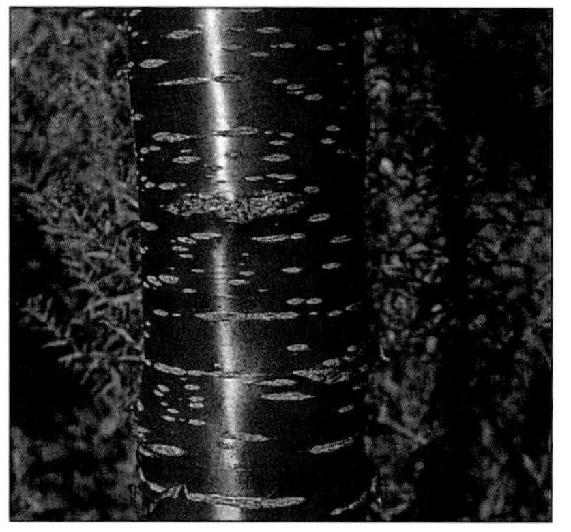

Prunus serrula Bark the colour of polished mahogany strikes a warm note in the winter landscape. 9 × 9m/30 × 30ft

Pinus pinea (Stone pine) Wonderfully tactile, bark such as this demands attention. 10 × 10m/33 × 33ft

◆ *Before planting any tree always ascertain its ultimate height and spread.*

Acer capillipes A snake bark maple suitable for smaller gardens. 9 × 9m/30 × 30ft

Acer griseum Another small tree whose burnished, peeling bark glows in winter sunshine. 8 × 6m/26 × 20ft

***Euonymus fortunei* 'Silver Queen'**
The creamy white variegation has a wonderfully wintery appearance which, later in the year, would be a perfect cool foil for hot perennials. For golden variegation, tinged bronzy-pink by cold, grow the smaller *E. fortunei* 'Emerald 'n' Gold'. E, 1 × 1.5m/3 × 5ft

WINTER SHRUBS

Imagine the garden filled with deliciously scented flowers throughout the darkest winter months. Such pleasures are easily realized by growing some of the winter-flowering shrubs. Positioned close to an outside door, or along a much frequented path where the fragrant flowers can easily and often be appreciated, these shrubs will be a source of enjoyment for weeks on end.

Others may be grown simply for the effect of foliage. Evergreens are valuable at all times of the year, never more so than in wintertime. Variegated leaves, particularly, glow when caught by the rays of a weak sun and look wonderfully vibrant seen against a dark background.

Cut both foliage and flower spikes to take indoors for a winter arrangement. Flowers cut in bud will rapidly open in a warm room to fill it with their scent.

Structure, in the form of trees, shrubs, hedges, walls and fences, indeed anything which affords permanent body and substance in the garden, is vitally important if the whole is not to appear flat and lifeless out of season. Not only do these provide a backdrop to the more ephemeral plantings of summer, they serve as well to maintain points of interest year round.

Many evergreens can be clipped into distinctive shapes. These yews, starkly etched by frost, are shaped to resemble giant chess pieces. An annual cut in late summer is sufficient to keep the outline.

***Hamamelis* × *intermedia* 'Pallida'** Spidery flowers, heavily scented, bloom on bare branches of the Chinese witch hazel in the first weeks of the year. This is a shrub deserving of space and patience, for it is very slow growing and will taken many years to reach its ultimate height and spread.
5 × 6m/16 × 20ft

◆ *Many named forms of witch hazel are grown, not least of which are* H. × intermedia *'Jelena', whose yellow flowers are suffused coppery-red, and* H. vernalis *'Sandra' for magnificent autumn colour.*

Sarcococca hookeriana var. ***digyna*** Edge a path with this Christmas box to enjoy the sweetness of its small white flowers all winter long. E, 1 × 1m/3 × 3ft

◆ *Contrast it with a carpet of the ground-hugging, evergreen* Pachysandra terminalis, *also with white flowers. To complete a green winter garden, include a plant of* Skimmia *'Kew Green' and, for a total relief of texture and form, the strappy* Cordaline australis, *though this is not reliably hardy.*

Ilex aquifolium **'Ferox Argentea'** This holly positively sparkles with its green leaves deeply edged in cream. Unusually, the prickles cover the entire leaf surface. E, 2.4 × 2.4m/8 × 8ft

◆ *Many hollies will lend themselves to being trained against a wall or support to form a dense screen.*

Chimonanthus praecox Aptly named wintersweet. Fragrant flowers produced from winter to early spring. ❍, 2.4 × 3m/ 8 × 10ft

Clematis cirrhosa An evergreen clematis producing small bell-shaped flowers, spotted on the inside, in late winter. E, 2 × 1m/ 6 × 3ft

Hedera helix **'Goldheart'** Use ivies to clothe unsightly or uninteresting surfaces. Some leaves will from time to time revert and should be cut out. E, 9m/30ft

***Pieris japonica* 'Mountain Fire'** New shoots of intense scarlet make this an exciting shrub to include in the winter border. It needs acidic soil. E, ◐, 3 × 3m/ 10 × 10ft

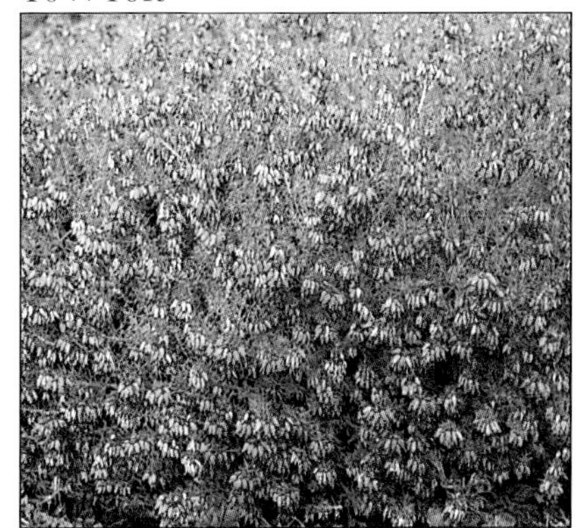

***Erica carnea* 'Myretoun Ruby'** All the winter-flowering heathers will tolerate alkaline soil. Heathers will benefit from cutting back hard after flowering. E, 30 × 45cm/12 × 18in

Lonicera fragrantissima Heavily perfumed flowers in winter. Later somewhat dull foliage can be enlivened with a mid-season clematis. 3 × 3m/10 × 10ft

Daphne odora Nothing can compare with the sweet, delicate perfume of the daphnes. Lovely, slow-growing shrubs ideally suited to small gardens. E, 1.5 × 1.5m/5 × 5ft

◆ *Daphnes will, for no apparent reason, often die when still young shrubs. There is nothing for it but to replant.*

Imaginative use has been made here of winter-flowering pansies. This showy display will remain eye-catching for many weeks, even during prolonged periods of cold.

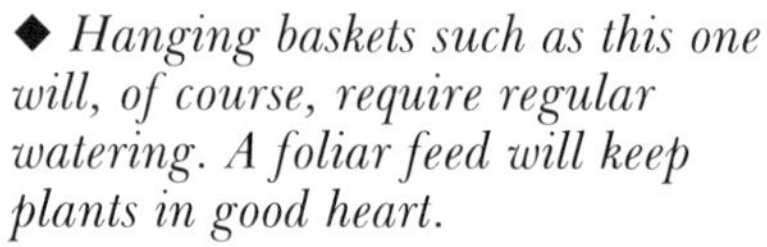

◆ *Hanging baskets such as this one will, of course, require regular watering. A foliar feed will keep plants in good heart.*

Outstandingly stylish, bay lends itself to clipping into shapes. Here it is made into a standard tree which would look most elegant next to a doorway.

Young shrubs may be used most effectively in containers, as this window box demonstrates. Variegated foliage lightens the scheme and is suggestive of warmer days.

Light pruning from time to time will keep shrubs to size and in shape. Eventually they may, of course, outgrow their spaces when they should be replaced.

Compost should not be allowed to dry out. The addition of a liquid feed when watering will be beneficial to the plants.

Winter is no reason why window boxes and containers should not look as attractive and colourful as in summertime. Here attention has been given to form and texture to create an interesting and balanced display. Shaped box balls contrast with the loose form of the trailing ivies whilst heathers, *Erica carnea*, contribute a splash of warm and welcome colour. Small, spring-flowering bulbs could well be included to extend the period of interest.

PRUNING CLEMATIS
Prune late-flowering clematis, such as late large-flowered hybrids, viticella and texensis groups, at this time. Reduce last year's growth to strong buds just above the base.

Early-flowering clematis, such as the montanas (see p. 81), require little or no pruning. Immediately after flowering, reduce surplus growth and cut out any weak stems or dead wood.

Clematis flowering before midsummer should for the most part be lightly pruned. This involves checking the growth of lengthy spurs, pruning any tangled stems and removing old flower heads.

PRUNING

Towards the very end of this period, in early spring, start pruning the fully hardy shrubs that bloomed in the late summer of the previous year such as *Buddleja davidii*, *Hypericum calycinum* (Rose of Sharon) and *Spiraea douglasii*. Leave less hardy shrubs such as ceanothus, fuchsia, hydrangea until any danger of severe frosts is past (see April, page 61).

Trees to be pruned, among them those grown for the effect of their new foliage, include: *Acer pensylvanicum* 'Erythrocladum', *A. negundo* 'Flamingo', *Ailanthus, Eucalyptus, Paulownia* (shown above), *Platanus* (plane), *Populus* (poplar), and *Tilia* (lime).

In the kitchen garden prune fruit trees and apply a winter wash of tar oil. Similarly, spray peach trees against peach leaf curl. Fruiting bushes (blueberries, currants and gooseberries) should be pruned and autumn-fruiting raspberries cut to the ground.

After pruning has taken place, a routine mulch of good garden compost around the base of the plant will stimulate growth for the new season. At the same time check ties and stakes.

IN THE POTTING SHED
Jobs which have been put off in the past can be tackled now. A wet day is a good opportunity to sort through the potting shed to have everything in place and readiness for the new season. Use this time to service the lawn mower and oil and sharpen tools.

Indoors, order supplies such as weedkillers, sprays, fertilizers, seed and potting compost for spring use.

PLANNING THE YEAR
Freezing temperatures, biting winds, sleet and snow will deter even the most committed gardeners from venturing outside. These are times to retreat indoors, to seek inspiration for the months ahead from gardening books and nursery catalogues.

Now is the moment to plan changes and indulge new ideas. Perhaps the reshaping of a border, a new planting scheme or the installation of a pond. Whatever, planning of this kind, itself exciting and enjoyable, will ensure that the garden continues to evolve a distinctive and personal style.

CHECK LIST

- Flower indoor and tender plants in a warm conservatory (p.18).
- Grow trees and shrubs for winter effect and colour (pp.19, 20).
- Appraise the garden for form and structure (p.20).
- Plant window boxes and containers for seasonal colour (p.24).
- Carry out winter pruning (p.26).
- Apply winter wash and sprays to fruit trees (p.26).
- Check stakes and ties.
- Tidy and organize shed (p.27).
- Order supplies for the coming season (p.27).
- Plan changes and alterations to the garden (p.27).
- Plant summer-flowering bulbs (e.g. lilies) when the soil has warmed.
- Ensure you have taken precautions against cold weather (p.228).

PLANT DECIDUOUS TREES
Winter is the time to plant bare-rooted deciduous trees and shrubs if the ground is not frozen or too wet. Dig a sufficiently wide hole, insert a stake and then spread the roots out before firming soil over them.

MARCH

SPRING BEGINS in earnest this month with cheerful daffodils and early tulips playing a prominent part. As the weather improves and the soil warms, it seems as if nature herself is stirred into action. For the gardener it is the start of a busy period as the new season gets underway.

Newly planted trees and shrubs benefit from a top dressing of organic matter to assist establishment. Hedges, purchased bare root and planted in the autumn, should be checked. Firm any loose soil and lightly fork in a sprinkling of fish, blood and bone meal to promote growth.

In the vegetable garden there is still time to prepare the ground before the major plantings of next month. Shallots, onion sets and Jerusalem artichokes as well as garlic and early potatoes can all be set out now. Potatoes will, of course, need protection from frost.

***Tulipa kaufmanniana* 'Gaiety'** Short stems and wide open flowers exposed to the sun are a mark of the water lily tulips. Planted deeply they can remain in the ground to become a permanent feature year after year. More than any other variety, 'Gaiety' most closely resembles a water lily. 15cm/6in

◆ *All bulbs require good drainage. With heavy soils break up the base of the planting hole with a little horticultural grit. This is easily carried out with a hand fork.*

***Narcissus* 'Rip van Winkle'** This double daffodil is, on account of its small size, ideal for a rock or sink garden. It will increase steadily to form a drift. 15 × 15cm/6 × 6in

***Narcissus* 'Tête-à-Tête'** Low-growing daffodils have an attraction in as much as they withstand the wind. This one often has two trumpets to a single stem. 20 × 15cm/8 × 6in

***Narcissus* 'Thalia'** Tall-stemmed daffodils are, by tradition, yellow. The ice white of 'Thalia' looks wonderfully startling against a dark background. 30cm/1ft

◆ *Daffodils are well suited to a woodland situation or the very back of a border where they may be left to naturalize.*

SPRING BULBS

To enjoy the effect of massed bulbs now, it must be remembered that they need to be ordered in summer for autumn planting.

Rather than plant individually, which is very time consuming, dig holes sufficient to take a number. Groups of nine, eleven or more throughout a border will give both a full and natural impression.

After flowering dead head but allow foliage to wither.

Muscari neglectum Grape hyacinths will rapidly colonize an area. They make a splendid blue carpet to contrast with the yellows of spring. 10–15cm/4–6in

Narcissus lobularis Truly wild daffodils are seldom offered for sale in bulb catalogues. This small species daffodil is an excellent substitute for it is low-growing and tough, perfectly capable of blooming through snow.

An alternative would be *N. obvallaris*, slightly taller than *N. lobularis*, but one of the finest varieties for naturalizing in grass. 20cm/8in

THE WILD GARDEN

How evocative is the thought of a wild bank carpeted in moss through which grow tiny treasures of spring flowers. First would be aconites, followed by wild daffodils and wood anemones, cowslips and oxslips, celandines, clumps of primroses and, later, a haze of bluebells.

Such an idea is not as improbable as may at first appear. With a little imagination and ingenuity it should be possible to create a wild area in some corner of the garden.

***Scilla sibirica* 'Spring Beauty'** Impossible to resist. This delightful little squill of intense delphinium-blue is erect in form and, because of its sterility, is long-lasting in flower. An extravagant planting of this bulb will result in a charming show for years to come. As with all small bulbs, scatter first then plant to achieve a natural effect. 15cm/6in

Planting such a wild garden need not be too exact. The inclusion of a few cultivated forms of plant will in no way detract from the overall picture.

Cardamine, the delicate lady's smock of meadow and ditches, hepatica, galium, the sweet woodruff flowering in partial shade, scented violets and soft-coloured primulas would not be out of place. Neither would the snakeshead fritillary *Fritillaria meleagris*, to flower a little later on.

EARLY SPRING PERENNIALS

Borders at this stage of the year still look somewhat bare as the summer perennials have yet to come into proper growth. It is, therefore, important to cultivate plants which, alongside spring bulbs, will flower early. Many of these early perennials, such as the hellebores, the epimediums and the primulas, have attractive foliage which will remain looking good long after the flowers have faded and gone. Regular dead heading ensures that plants retain a freshness which is necessary to the overall appearance of the mixed border.

Primula denticulata Drumstick primulas are easy to grow in any soil which does not dry out completely in summer. 'Alba' is a white form. 30 × 30cm/1 × 1ft

◆ *Make room for generous clumps of polyanthus. These merry, multi-coloured plants are suitable either as spring bedding or planted permanently in semi-shade.*

***Primula* 'Dawn Ansell'** Double primulas enjoy well cultivated, rich soil and should be lifted and split regularly after flowering. 15 × 15cm/6 × 6in

Corydalis solida Intense violet-blue flowers. Plant in a position to allow for partial shade as the year progresses. ◐, 30 × 30cm/ 1 × 1ft

***Epimedium* × *youngianum* 'Niveum'** The delicate flowers rise from a base of fresh, new leaves. Old foliage should be removed immediately before flowering. 25 × 30cm/10in × 1ft

Anemone appenina Leave these lovely and easy rhizomes undisturbed to naturalize in a semi-shaded situation in well-enriched soil. Around the base of a tree or between shrubs they will form a low carpet. Usually blue, the white form 'Alba' is also available. 10 × 7.5cm/4 × 3in

◆ *Many plants, such as these anemones, thrive when grown in conditions where leafmould, well rotted manure or friable compost has been worked into the soil.*

***Ipheion uniflorum* 'Violaceum'** An absolutely charming front of border plant. 15 × 15cm/6 × 6in

◆ *Occasionally* Ipheion *will disappear for a season; the following year it will certainly reappear.*

SPRING DIVISIONS

The emergence of new basal leaves on later flowering perennials indicates a good time to divide and replenish.

Using a fork, lift plant and shake off excess soil. Either split into pieces by crossing over two forks placed in the middle of the plant or, more easily, divide into segments with a spade.

Discard the tired, woody centre retaining divisions of outer pieces. Replant with fresh compost and water in.

***Ranunculus ficaria* 'Brazen Hussy'** This lesser celandine is a good subject for the early spring wild garden. It dies down in late spring. 5 × 20cm/2 × 8in

Helleborus lividus* subsp. *corsicus The large clusters of pale green flowers on the Corsican hellebore begin in winter and continue into spring. ◐, 60 × 45cm/2ft × 18in

***Bergenia* 'Silberlicht'** Bergenias are valuable for their early spring flowers and their 'elephant ear' leaves all year. 30 × 50cm/12 × 20in

***Pulmonaria officinalis* 'Sissinghurst White'** Many of the lungworts are semi-evergreen. They grow in clumps and produce welcome flowers in blue, white or pink from late winter. ◐, 30 × 45cm/1 × 1½ft

◆ *Clumps of hellebores surrounded by lungworts make an excellent early spring combination. Both prefer semi-shade.*

Erythronium A genus that includes the pink dog's tooth violets, *E. dens-canis*. They are one of the prettiest and most graceful of all the early flowers. For successful cultivation they should be given moist, well drained soil in partial shade and left undisturbed to increase. ◐, 30 × 20cm/1ft × 8in

◆ *Bulb catalogues list a number of named varieties. These include 'Purple King', 'Rose Queen', 'Pagoda' and 'White Beauty'. Plant bulbs in the autumn for spring flowering.*

EARLY SPRING SHRUBS

Shrubs are the backbone of any mixed border and their framework contributes structure throughout the year.

Magnificent now is the large shrub or small tree, *Magnolia stellata*. This is one of the first magnolias to flower and an established plant will be literally covered in small, white stars.

For scent, the evergreen *Mahonia* × *media* 'Charity' is unrivalled, whilst the spectacular, near orange flowers of *Berberis darwinii* are bound to excite interest.

Forsythia Golden yellow flowers which should be pruned after flowering. Forsythia may be trained against a wall or planted as a hedge. 3 × 2m/10 × 6ft

***Rhododendron* 'Praecox'** An early-flowering hybrid rhododendron with soft, rosy-purple flowers and leaves which, when crushed, are aromatic. ◐, E, 1.2–2 × 1.2–2m/4–6 × 4–6ft

◆ *Rhododendrons, with few exceptions, require acidic soil, part shade and an annual mulch. Some deciduous varieties have striking autumn colour.*

Viburnum* × *burkwoodii Fragrant flowers, pink in bud opening to white, are set off by dark, shiny leaves which are felted on the underside. E, 2 × 2m/6 × 6ft

***Camellia* 'Water Lily'** Beautiful, spring flowering shrubs of which 'Water Lily' is one of the first. Camellias require acid or neutral soil in a position away from early morning sun. ◐, E, 2 × 2m/ 6 × 6ft

LAWN CARE

It would be foolish to suggest that the upkeep of a perfect lawn is simply a matter of mowing. However, by adopting a programme of routine maintenance, it should be possible to have a respectable lawn which will remain in condition throughout the year. A new lawn can be established at this time or in the autumn – see page 198 for details.

EARLY SPRING
- lightly rake grass to remove debris of winter
- first cut (choose a dry day and set the mower blades high)
- establish edges with half-moon
- apply moss kill

SPRING
- commence mowing and edging on a regular basis (keep up through summer and into autumn)
- apply feed and weed (repeat as necessary)

SUMMER
- spot treat persistent weeds
- apply nitrogen feed

AUTUMN
- scarify and spike compacted grass
- apply autumn feed (specifically chosen for slow release properties)
- final cut of grass
- keep off grass in frosty weather

MOWING STRIP

A lawn can be edged with flagstones or bricks so that plants in adjoining borders are able to spill over without damaging the grass or impeding mowing.

Repot plants
Repot plants with fresh compost to ensure that they are in good heart for the new season. A top dressing of horticultural grit will improve appearances.

Cut back ornamental grasses
All of the ornamental grasses, like this *Stipa tenuissima*, will remain attractive through the winter. Reduced to ground level in early spring, they will rapidly renew.

Beware of *Phalaris arundinacea* 'Picta'. Commonly known as gardeners' garters, this grass is too invasive for the average garden.

Pruning roses
Prune roses according to type (for rose types see June, pages 112–119) in the early part of the year by cutting to an outward facing bud. Complete by feeding and mulching.

HYBRID TEA ROSES Reduce all growth to approximately 30cm/1ft above ground level. Entirely remove diseased or damaged stems.

FLORIBUNDA ROSES As for Hybrid Teas but retain strong side shoots to around 15cm/6in.

SHRUB ROSES Cut away weak and damaged stems. Remove several centre branches at base level to open up the bush. Shorten other shoots by about one third.

CLIMBING ROSES Cut back side branches and tie in strong new shoots.

RAMBLER ROSES Check ties on new shoots. Any pruning should have been carried out immediately after flowering (see August, page 185).

MINIATURE/PATIO ROSES Generally cut out any dead, diseased or twiggy growth. Periodically open up the bushes.

PRUNE FOR WINTER COLOUR
Salix alba vitellina 'Britzensis' pictured in early spring. Pollarding of this willow has taken place and all the previous year's growth has been reduced to a few main stems.

The same shrub in winter, its warm orange colour reflected in water.

Many shrubs may be enjoyed throughout the winter months on account of their brightly coloured bark. Not least of these are the willows and dogwoods. Indeed, severe pollarding encourages strong, new growth which results in maximum colour effect.

This treatment may also be used deliberately to restrict the size of a tree or shrub to fit a particular position in a smaller garden.

CHECK LIST

- Top dress newly planted trees and shrubs (p.28).
- Plant shallots and onion sets. Sow early potatoes (p.28).
- Dead head early flowering bulbs (p.29).
- Plant a wild garden (pp. 30–31).
- Lift and divide summer flowering perennials (p.33).
- Plant new borders.
- Start programme of lawn care (p.37).
- Repot container plants (p.38).
- Cut back ornamental grasses (p.38).
- Prune roses (p.38).
- Pollard shrubs and trees grown for winter colour (p.39).
- Continue pruning fully hardy late-summer flowering shrubs (p.26).
- Under glass, start overwintered tubers of dahlias by watering and bringing them into the light.
- Protect new shoots from slugs, particularly herbaceous plants and clematis.

SOW HALF HARDY ANNUALS
In preparation for summer bedding schemes half hardy annuals should be sown under glass in seed trays or pans. Compost should be moist and firm before seeds are scattered. Seeds, unless very small, should be covered with a thin layer of compost. As soon as seedlings break through, remove glass. Prick out when first leaves have formed. Harden off.

APRIL

APRIL MARKS THE START of a period of feverish activity in the garden. Winter wet is past and the drying winds of March make the ground, at least on the surface, dry, crumbly and workable. Balmy days promote weed growth which, tackled now, will eliminate much work later on. Small weed seedlings are easily destroyed with the hoe if conditions are right. More persistent, perennial weeds should be dug out by hand whilst troublesome infestations may be attacked if necessary with the use of a selective weed killer. Bulbous plants provide much of the colour in the borders. Massed displays convey an appearance of fullness which is welcome at a time when many herbaceous perennials remain dormant. By carefully mixing daffodils and tulips, as well as other bulbs, it should be possible to have a continuous display for several weeks to come. Bulbs which have flowered earlier on should be dead headed and allowed to die down.

This charming mixture of pink hyacinths and white violas demonstrates the effect of mass planting. The success lies as much in the simplicity of the combination as in the number of plants. Bedding schemes of this kind are labour intensive for once the flowering period is over the whole border will need to be replanted.

◆ *When obtaining hyacinth bulbs in the autumn avoid purchasing those intended for forcing in pots indoors. Those for outdoor use are considerably cheaper.*

Wallflowers (***Cheiranthus***) are one of the mainstays of all spring bedding. Here they are partnered with tulips to produce a sunny, eye-catching display. They need to be sown in late summer in readiness to be set out in their flowering positions during the autumn. 30 × 30cm/1 × 1ft

◆ *Bedding of this kind is probably most suited to a more formal situation where other plantings will not detract from the overall effect.*

Tulipa saxatilis A species tulip often carrying two or more blooms on each stem. Named the rock tulip, it is an excellent choice for the rockery. 15cm/6in

◆ *All the species tulips, once planted, may be left undisturbed to establish themselves.*

***Tulipa* 'Apeldoorn'** One of the Darwin hybrid tulips which are noted for the brilliance of their blooms and long-lasting qualities. 60 × 20cm/2ft × 8in

Leucojum vernum The spring snowflake closely resembles the earlier flowering snowdrop. Dainty flowers, similar to small bells, are beautifully tipped with green or yellow. If left alone, in time *Leucojum* will increase, particularly when established in peaty soil which remains moist.

An attractive composition would be to allow them to drift among hellebores where they would enjoy the same conditions. 20 × 10cm/8 × 4in

To grow daffodils in this number in this way must, for many, remain a dream. The reality requires considerable space and a formidable number of years to allow for naturalization. However, pleasing results may easily be achieved by planting bold, generous clumps throughout the border where the eye will automatically be drawn from one to the next.

Fritillaria meleagris These snakeshead fritillaries with their unusual markings do best when left to naturalize in grass as shown here. Indeed, they seem to resent border cultivation and do far less well in open ground. Even quite a small area of lawn could be designated as a wild flower meadow providing that grass cutting is delayed until the flowers have had a chance to seed. 25cm/10in

Fritillaria imperialis Crown imperials must surely rank amongst the aristocrats of the spring border. Flowers, in red, orange or yellow, form a ring at the top of stately stems and are surmounted by a tuft of leaves. Bulbs are best planted on their sides on a bed of coarse sand or grit. Failure to flower may be because of a lack of potash fertilizer which is necessary for the formation of flower buds. After planting dress with sulphate of potash and apply each year at a rate of 25g/1oz per square metre/yard. 1.5m × 30cm/5 × 1ft

Enjoy these delightful, unassuming spring flowers in any semi-shaded situation. Grow all members of the primula family in humus-rich moisture retentive soil. 15 × 15cm/6 × 6in

◆ *Polyanthus should be lifted and divided periodically. Late spring, when flowering is complete, is the best time for this.*

***Primula* 'Guinevere'** One of many attractively coloured primulas which are, once more, fashionable to grow. Plant them in dappled shade. 15 × 15cm/6 × 6in

Lamium orvala Unlike so many of the lamiums which spread outwards to cover the ground, this one is clump forming. Rose-pink flowers are set off by textured leaves which remain fresh for a long period. In the autumn look for self-sown seedlings close to the parent plant. 60 × 30cm/2 × 1ft

◆ *Of similar habit to* L. orvala *is* L. galeobdolon *'Hermann's Pride'. However, this form has distinctive, silvery markings on the leaves.*

***Primula* 'Hose-in-Hose'** At first glance this appears as a traditional primrose, but the flowers are in fact carried above a fascinating ruff of miniature leaves. 10 × 10cm/4 × 4in

***Primula* 'Dusky Lady'** The appeal of this aptly named primula lies in the deep wine colour of the flowers and the dark, shaded leaves. 15 × 15cm/6 × 6in

***Veronica peduncularis* 'Georgia Blue'** An absolute must. Flowering in the main throughout the spring, 'Georgia Blue' will carry some blooms in each month of the year. E, 15 × 30m/6in × 1ft

Arum creticum This showy species of arum with creamy-white spathes and a noticeable, pencil-like spadix makes a spectacular spring display. 30 × 30cm/1 × 1ft

◆ *Tubers should be planted in autumn in full sun and given reasonable drainage. Do not disturb unless to propagate by division of offsets.*

Uvularia grandiflora The bellwort is seldom seen in gardens which is surprising as, given reasonable conditions, it is not at all difficult. Peaty soil, which does not dry out, and some partial shade are all that is required. ◐, 30 × 30cm/1 × 1ft

◆ *Poor soil may be improved and conditioned by forking in liberal quantities of leaf mould made over the winter period.*

Doronicum columnae The leopard's bane is an old-fashioned plant producing bright yellow early flowers. 45 × 45cm/1½ × 1½ft

Brunnera macrophylla The Siberian bugloss bears forget-me-not flowers over good green foliage. ◐, 45 × 60cm/1½ × 2ft

◆ *This is a good ground-cover plant for semi-shade.*

The Water Garden in Spring

In many respects the pondside at this time of year is at its best. Marginal plantings, now in flower, have the space to look showy whereas later on growth becomes so lush as to be in danger of obscuring individual plants. Always, of course, it is important to mask the edges of a pond, particularly those which are of preformed construction or make use of a liner. Plants which come into leaf early on, near evergreen grasses and thoughtfully chosen ferns, are ideal for this purpose.

For colour, look to the marsh marigolds, the skunk cabbages, the umbrella plant, *Darmera peltata*, cardamines, primulas, early saxifrages and ranunculus.

Lysichiton camtschatcensis A cousin of *L. americanus*, this has spathes that are white rather than yellow and appear slightly later. 75 × 60cm/2½ × 2ft

◆ *Skunk cabbages will come readily from seed though it will take several years to produce a flowering plant.*

Caltha palustris The marsh marigold will flourish wherever the soil remains moist and is therefore good for the edge of the pond or the bog garden. ❍, 30 × 40cm/1 × 1½ft

◆ C. palustris *'Flore Pleno' is a fine double form with pompom type flower heads. Both will disappear completely later in the year.*

***Dicentra* 'Bacchanal'** Finely cut leaves and a dramatic, deep wine-red flower make this a most striking dicentra. Perfect with water, dicentras will succeed in any fertile garden soil. 45 × 30cm/1½ × 1ft

Arabis caucasica The intense white flowers of this rockery plant show up well against the dark evergreen foliage. Arabis will flourish in most situations and its trailing habit is useful for tumbling over low walls. After flowering dead head and cut back any excessive or unwanted growth. 15 × 30cm/6in × 1ft

THE ROCK GARDEN IN SPRING

So many alpines are spring-flowering it is no surprise that the rock garden, traditional home of small plants which might otherwise become lost, should be full of colour and interest at this time of year.

The cultivation of these miniature perennials is not difficult. For most, the essential requirement is the provision of good drainage. This may be achieved by incorporating generous amounts of horticultural grit with the compost into the planting hole. A sleeve of grit spread around the neck of the plant will further assist drainage as well as creating a trim appearance. It should be remembered that wet, causing rot, is far more likely to be the cause of the death of a plant than intense cold.

Of course the rock garden does not have to be limited to flowering alpines. Tiny ferns, dwarf, slow growing conifers, diminutive bulbs, even small-scale deciduous trees are all worthy of a place. Recognition of the importance of scale is, naturally, crucial to harmony, and anything eventually outgrowing its allocated space should be removed.

***Tulipa* 'Purissima'** Fosteriana tulips are noted for the magnificence of their oriental colours and create a startling picture when planted in groups. The milky white flowers of 'Purissima' are a sport of the well known 'Madame Lefeber', the red of which is quite different from any similar shade in tulips. 40 × 20cm/16 × 8in

◆ *Other exciting Fosteriana tulips are 'Cantate', a vermillion red, 'Summit', a mimosa yellow, and 'Orange Emperor', the colour of freshly pulled carrots.*

Pulsatilla vulgaris **Flowering at Easter, the Pasque flower is richly coloured deep purple with a harvest yellow eye. After the flowers are over they are replaced with wonderful, silky seedheads. If these are left, small seedlings will develop around the parent plant. 30 × 30cm/1 × 1ft**

◆ P. vulgaris alba *and* rubra *are white and red forms. All profit from sharp drainage.*

Aubrieta deltoidea Everyone is familiar with this spring carpeter for its loves to scramble over rocks, overrun inclines and creep into nooks and crannies. In fact it will root in the poorest of soils and will happily grow in the crevices of a dry stone wall or in crumbling mortar.
○, 5 × 45cm/2in × 1½ft

◆ *Immediately after flowering cut back hard. Do not be afraid to remove all the foliage as well as the dead flowers. In a very short time aubrieta will replenish itself and form an attractive, nicely shaped mound for the remainder of the season.*

Alyssum saxatile Smothered in egg yolk-yellow flowers, alyssum will flourish in drought conditions, indeed preferring a dry spot in infertile soil. For this reason they are often to be seen in partnership with aubrieta growing out of walls or in other seemingly inhospitable situations. ❍, 15 × 30cm/6in × 1ft

***Sanguinaria canadensis* 'Plena'** Bloodwort possesses charmingly shaped, blue-green leaves from which emerge solitary flowers of the purest of whites. ◐, 10cm/4in

Euphorbia myrsinites The principal attraction of this ground-hugging spurge must be its cool, glaucous foliage with whorls of lime flowers at the tips. ❍, E, 15 × 60cm/6in × 2ft

***Dicentra* 'Spring Morning'** Such appealing, finely-cut, fern-like foliage makes the pale pinky flowers an additional bonus. This is one of the loveliest of dicentras, enjoying a lengthy flowering period, and would team beautifully with mid-season tulips such as 'Grevel' or 'New Design'. 45 × 45cm/1½ × 1½ft

Viola labradorica An enchanting little viola whose purplish leaves in cold weather become quite, quite dark. Allow it to seed through the border.
10 × 30cm/4in × 1ft

***Anemone nemorosa* 'Robinsoniana'** Like all wood anemones, this one will naturalize in conditions of partial shade and where the soil is humus-rich. ◐, 15 × 30cm/6in × 1ft

SPRING SHRUBS AND TREES

Although the nights may still be cold, warmer days and seasonal showers act as a catalyst to bring trees and shrubs into leaf and, in many instances, flower. Many of the evergreen shrubs flower from now onwards. Among these are camellias, whose glossy leaves are a perfect foil to waxy blooms, some viburnums, early rhododendrons and sweetly scented osmanthus. Flowering trees include a large number of prunus, noble magnolias, and willows with their fascinating catkins. Trees like *Prunus subhirtella* 'Autumnalis', which will have been in flower during mild spells throughout the winter, are now a sheet of lovely, semi-double white flowers. Use the area at the base of these early trees and shrubs to grow small, spring bulbs. Some of the deliciously fragrant jonquil narcissi, such as 'Baby Moon' or 'Suzy', *Fritillaria michailovskyi*, or the powder puff heads of the feather hyacinth, *Muscari plumosum*, would all be suitable.

Salix lanata Even the smallest garden could accommodate the slow growing, woolly willow. Silver-grey, felted leaves complement the yellowish spring catkins. This dwarf tree is a worthy subject for the rock garden providing, as with all willows, the soil is not allowed to dry out. Spray against sawfly in spring. 1 × 1m/3 × 3ft

***Acer pseudoplatanus* 'Brilliantissimum'** New foliage, the colour of the freshest of shrimps, cannot be ignored. This small tree in new leaf is quite spectacular, a dazzling addition to any garden. As the year progresses so the colour fades to yellow-green, turning once more to coppery brown before leaf fall. 6 × 7m/20 × 23ft

***Chaenomeles speciosa* 'Nivalis'** Flowers of japonica are followed by large yellow fruits from which are made traditional quince jelly. This white form is but one of many varieties, red being more common. Of the named reds, *C.* × *superba* 'Knap Hill Scarlet' and 'Rowallane' are possibly best known and most widely grown. 2.4 × 5m/8 × 16ft

Camellia **'Nobilissima'** All camellias will benefit from an annual top dressing of leaf mould, decayed manure or suitable vegetable matter. ◐, E, 3 × 2m/10 × 6ft

Camellia **'Galaxie'** Those who garden on chalk or limestone will be restricted to growing camellias, such as this pretty pink one, in pots or tubs. ◐, E, 2 × 2m/6 × 6ft

◆ *Ideally potting soil should be made up of 2 parts of lime-free loam, 1 of moss peat, 1 of leaf mould and 1 of coarse sand or grit.*

***Magnolia* × *loebneri* 'Leonard Messel'** Spring flowering magnolias are surely one of the joys of this time of year. Hardy, largely tolerant of alkaline soil and fairly slow growing, they are a natural choice for the majority of gardens. 'Leonard Messel', illustrated here, flowers on bare wood with lilac-pink blooms, deeper in bud. ❍, 8 × 6m/ 26 × 20ft

◆ *Sadly a late frost can disfigure the flowers of magnolias, causing them to go an unsightly brown. Fortunately this has no adverse effect in the long-term.*

Magnolia* × *soulangeana Flowers are tulip-shaped, principally white flushed with rose-purple. This form, 'Burgundy', will, as others of the type, flower whilst still quite young. ❍, 6 × 6m/20 × 20ft

Viburnum* × *juddii Include this fairly compact viburnum in the border not least for its beautifully scented flowers. 1.5 × 1.5/5 × 5ft

◆ *Viburnums are not difficult to grow and are tolerant of a wide range of conditions. Avoid planting in soil which becomes water-logged in winter.*

***Prunus* 'Pink Shell'** One of the ornamental cherries whose pale pink blossom is softer, and more pleasing, than some of the stronger pinks which are often grown. 9 × 8m/30 × 26ft

***Rhododendron* Hybrid 'Lem's Cameo'** Hybrid rhododendrons are generally characterized by plentiful foliage, firm flower trusses and total hardiness. Newer introductions may, in certain circumstances, prove less tolerant to extreme conditions. 'Lem's Cameo' flowers before the main rhododendron flowering period of May. E, 2 × 2m/6 × 6ft

◆ *If old plants of the hardy hybrid rhododendrons become leggy, hard prune during the winter months.*

***Salix caprea* 'Kilmarnock'** Weeping willows have a universal appeal. Unfortunately, as many gardeners know to their cost, they grow to a size which renders them unsuitable for garden cultivation. Not so the Kilmarnock willow which is compact in growth and makes an excellent specimen tree. 2 × 2m/6 × 6ft

Berberis darwinii Berberis are such versatile shrubs. *B. darwinii* provides flower in spring, interesting form throughout the summer and berries in autumn. E, 4 × 4m/13 × 13ft

***Skimmia japonica* 'Rubella'** All winter this shrub will be a mass of red buds, opening at this time to white, yellow anthered flowers. E, 1.5 × 1.5m/5 × 5ft

Osmanthus delavayi Plant in an enclosed space to appreciate fully the wonderful scent of this spring-flowering, glossy-leafed shrub. E, 3 × 3m/10 × 10ft

PLANT PURCHASING

A visit to a garden centre or nursery at this time of year will reveal an often bewildering array of trees, shrubs, herbaceous perennials, alpines and vegetable seedlings. The majority of these will be offered for sale in pots as container-grown. This is a convenient and reliable way of buying plants.

Throughout the winter, indeed from late autumn, it is possible to purchase plants bare-root. Trees, plants for hedging and roses are typically sold in this manner. It is, of course, much cheaper to buy in this way and is completely satisfactory as long as the plants are dormant. Do not purchase plants being sold as bare-root if there are signs of buds breaking into leaf. See page 27 for planting bare-root.

EARLY CLEMATIS

It is not just their lovely colours but the nodding habit of their flower heads which make the alpina and macropetala clematis so appealing. On the left is *C. alpina*, on the right *C. macropetala* 'Blue Bird'.

These are clematis to scramble into the lower branches of trees and shrubs, to tumble over low retaining walls or to grow in pots and containers. Both types will respond to pegging down to the surface of the soil to form a colourful and effective ground cover.

Pruning is simply limited to removing unwanted growth and cutting out any weak or dead stems. Periodically no harm will be done if the whole plant is cut back to ground level. All clematis respond to an annual feed of well rotted compost or manure applied around the base of the plant. This is best carried out in late winter.

***Clematis macropetala* 'Markham's Pink'** These sugary pink flowers would look gorgeous in association with many of the spring flowering bulbs. For absolute elegance, seek out *C. macropetala* 'Snowbird' with outer sepals of pure white, the inner cluster of greenish-white. It is not uncommon for the macropetalas to produce a small flush of flowers in autumn. 1.8m/6ft

◆ *Macropetala and alpina clematis do equally well in both sun or partial shade although the former do prefer a shadier aspect.*

TENDER PERENNIALS

Many border perennials which are inclined to be tender are best left until now to be cut back. By leaving the previous year's growth in place until spring, the plant is afforded a little extra protection from winter frost, wind and wet. This simple delaying tactic should ensure that winter losses are kept to a minimum.

Among those perennials which would benefit from this treatment are all the penstemons, diascias, hardy fuchsias and border osteospermums.

Illustrated here is *Penstemon glaber*. This is one of the smaller growing penstemons, enjoying a long flowering season from early summer onwards. E, ❍, 60 × 60cm/2 × 2ft

DIVISIONS

Herbaceous perennials in need of division which were not tackled in March may still be lifted and divided this month.

April is by tradition the time of year when asters, Michaelmas daisies, are divided. In fact it is important to carry this out on a regular basis or clumps will become woody, dying out completely in the centre with a subsequent loss of flower.

Aster novi-belgii 'Goliath', shown here, will flower from late summer into autumn in an open, sunny situation. ❍, 1.2m × 45cm/4 × 1½ft

PLANTING EVERGREENS

April is an ideal month in which to plant evergreen trees and shrubs. The soil has had a chance to warm and is still moist from the recent rain of late winter and early spring.

Choose a time when the ground is neither frozen nor waterlogged. Prepare the planting area well by removing any perennial weeds and large stones and digging in a generous quantity of garden compost or peat. Finally, lightly fork in a little bone meal.

Dig a hole which is large enough to accommodate the roots of the plant and line the base with a good measure of planting compost. Before removing the plant from its container, or unpacking the root ball if ball-rooted, water well.

Insert a stake and then place the plant in position. Tease out any tangled roots and infill with planting medium. Firm down to eliminate pockets of air but do not compact. Keep watered in dry periods.

SOW HARDY ANNUALS

Hardy annuals, like this clarkia, may be sown during April in open ground where they are to flower.

With a few exceptions, hardy annuals require very little in the way of specially cultivated or enriched soil. The surface should be made level, finely raked and watered, if dry, in advance of sowing. Seed should be sown thinly and lightly covered with finely sifted soil.

Once germination has occurred, seedlings should be thinned out to allow plants to develop.

PROTECT SEEDLINGS
Given mild weather seed will not take long to germinate and appear. Here young pea seedlings are putting on rapid growth and will soon need the support of twigs to assist development. Spring crops are particularly vulnerable to decimation by birds. The protection of netting, or even thread criss-crossed over the crop, is advised.

During the month check the setting of fruit and spray if necessary against pests and diseases.

THE KITCHEN GARDEN
Of all months, April is one of the busiest in the kitchen garden if there is to be a succession of vegetables throughout the year. Beds will have been prepared over winter, during which time weeding, digging and manuring will have taken place. Ground should now be raked to a fine tilth in readiness for seed-sowing or planting out of seedlings.

In today's gardens space is at a premium. For this reason it is useful, and efficient, to plan which vegetables are to be grown and to place together those which have similar nutritional needs. In the main, it is sensible to vary from year to year the beds in which crops are grown.

Sowing should begin in the open on fairly dry soil which has had time to warm after winter. In order to obtain a succession of vegetables, and to avoid gluts, it is wise to sow successive small quantities so that crop may follow crop. Always sow in drills rather than broadcast seed. Water if the weather is dry, especially whilst seedlings are tender.

Thinning will be unnecessary where seeds are sown thinly; otherwise thin according to the distances advised for each vegetable.

Outdoors, the following may be sown: broad beans, beetroot, carrots, chicory, leeks, lettuce, spring onions, parsley, parsnip, peas, radish, spinach and Swiss chard. Of the brassicas, broccoli, cabbage, kale, swede and turnip may all be sown. Aubergine, French beans, celery, sweetcorn and outdoor tomatoes will need to be sown in heat or under protection.

Finally, artichokes, main-crop potatoes and strawberry runners may be planted out.

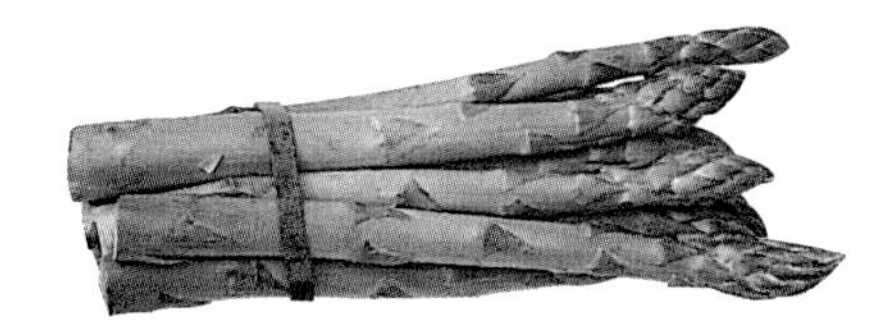

CULTIVATING ASPARAGUS
Asparagus is an absolute luxury, one of the most delightful of vegetables and never cheap to buy. For these reasons it is well worth taking a little trouble to establish and grow.

Asaparagus beds should occupy a sunny, open position. Soil should be deeply dug incorporating copious amounts of strawy manure for enrichment and drainage.

One or two year-old crowns should be obtained and planted during this month. Roots should be spead out and covered in good soil. Plants should be set in rows about 30cm/1ft apart. Dress in early spring each year with well rotted dung. Cropping should not take place until plants are three years old.

PROPAGATING DAHLIAS
The easiest method of propagation is to place overwintered tubers in March or April in shallow boxes of moist compost in a warm place. Quite quickly a number of strong shoots should appear. Detach these and set out in pots to grow on. After one season, treat as old tubers.

CHECK LIST

- Lift and divide polyanthus after flowering (p.44).
- Cultivate spring flowering alpines for the rock garden (p.48).
- Top dress camellias (p.54).
- Complete bare root plantings (p.56).
- Cut back tender perennials (p.58).
- Divide asters (p.58).
- Plant evergreen trees and shrubs (p.59).
- Sow hardy annuals in situ (p.59).
- Sow vegetable seeds (p.60).
- Establish an asparagus bed (p.61).
- Propagate dahlias (p.61).
- Prune early-flowering shrubs like *Berberis*, *Forsythia* and *Spiraea* immediately after flowering.
- Prune less hardy shrubs like *Ceanothus*, *Fuchsia*, *Hydrangea*.
- Mulch beds to help eliminate weeds and conserve moisture.

PLANTING WATER LILIES
Aquatic planting baskets, obtainable from good garden centres, are the easiest and most practical means of planting water lilies. These are open sided to allow for the expansion of the root system and are simply filled with a good growing medium into which the lily is planted.

Planting depths will depend upon the size of the lily. Miniature lilies may be planted in no more than 23cm/9in of water whilst small-growing ones will be happy in 30cm/1ft. Medium-growing lilies will need up to 45cm/1½ft, the most vigorous as much as 1m/3ft.

Thalictrum aquilegiifolium An excellent border plant which will, in time, form a substantial clump. Mauve, pink or white frothy flowers are carried above ferny foliage, not dissimilar in appearance to that of an aquilegia, hence the name. 1.2m × 60cm/4 × 2ft

MAY

MAY is one of the loveliest of months. The magic of spring peaks and everywhere gardens rejoice in a surfeit of colour and that first, wonderful freshness which embraces town and country alike. Borders, previously pocketed with bare soil, burgeon with the unstoppable growth of perennials many of which, until now, have had life checked by the uncertainties and vagaries of April weather. This is the month of those splendid fillers, forget-me-nots, honesty, grannies' bonnets which, left to seed, contribute to an air of plenty and fullness to which all gardeners aspire. Weeds remain a potential problem. Encouraged by ideal growing conditions they will, unless seriously arrested with hoe or hand fork, take hold. Any mulch applied last month will help control them, as will ground-cover plants.

Aquilegia vulgaris Columbines should be allowed to seed throughout the border where they will produce some outrageous crosses in a wide range of hues. Long spurs and finely cut leaves contribute a sense of lightness and airiness. Following flowering (and seeding if required), cut to ground level. Within a short time a fresh mound of foliage will appear. Look out for named varieties such as 'Nora Barlow' and 'Magpie'. 1m × 45cm/3 × 1½ft

A beautifully co-ordinated, colour-themed May border which demonstrates a sensitive use of flower, form and foliage. Drifts of forget-me-nots are complemented by taller growing columbines whilst the Welsh poppy, *Meconopsis cambrica*, provides a yellow accent throughout. This in turn picks up the gold of the hosta leaves and will as surely tone with the *Hemerocallis*, day lily, which is about to flower.

Borders, such as this one, which possess an air of casual accident are, in fact, quite carefully and skilfully contrived and demand a high degree of plant knowledge.

Armeria maritima Thrift will grow, as in the wild, in poor soil provided it is given reasonable drainage. Dead heading will result in continuous flowering. ○, E, 10 × 20cm/4 × 8in

Saxifraga* × *urbium London Pride can make a splendid edging to a path and is tolerant of both sun and shade. Cut off the spent heads to keep the plants looking neat. E, 30 × 30cm/1ft × 1ft

***Phlox carolina* 'Bill Baker'** An invaluable, early flowering phlox which is most useful for infilling at the front of the border. 30 × 30cm/1 × 1ft

Lunaria annua alba, white honesty, Welsh poppies and faithful forget-me-nots combine here to give a flavour of the traditional cottage garden which is so much admired. All these hardy annuals and biennials are self-sown and once established in the garden require little, if any attention. Any unwanted seedlings may very easily be removed.

Euphorbia polychroma Bracts of greenish-yellow rise above a compact mound of foliage to dominate this spring spurge. Cut down in autumn but avoid skin contact with the poisonous sap of all euphorbias. 45 × 60cm/1½ × 2ft

***Euphorbia griffithii* 'Fireglow'** Startling orange-red bracts certainly make a dramatic statement when planted in bold clumps. Keep watch, though, for this euphorbia likes to run and is very capable of exceeding its allocated space. ❍, 1m × 75cm/3 × 2½ft

Lunaria annua alba Biennial white honesty sparkles wherever it chooses to place itself. Later the flat, translucent seed pods will be in demand for indoor decoration. 1m × 45cm/3 × 1½ft

◆ *Familiar in the late spring will be* Lunaria annua *with its purple, scented flowers. It too will seed around.*

***Bellis* 'Medici Rose'** In this case the double daisy is partnered with star of Bethlehem – an original and striking display. 15 × 23cm/6 × 9in

◆ *Schemes like this need to be planned well in advance so that plants have time to establish.*

Centaurea montana Cornflowers belong to that old-fashioned group of flowers which are always deserving of a place in the garden. 45 × 60cm/1½ × 2ft

Planting for effect

All too often the mistake is made of setting out a single plant in a border where several are required if a total effect is to be achieved.

Experience shows that blocks, or ribbons, of the same plant in a border are a certain way of creating impact. Contrasts, either of colour, form or texture, are likely to be all the greater if plantings are generous and carried out with at least a sense of plenteous abandon.

An odd number of plants placed together is more convincing than an even one, although once above a dozen or more it probably does not matter.

This planting of *Veronica gentianoides* 'Tissington White' underlines the idea. 45 × 45cm/1½ × 1½ft

Gentiana acaulis Unforgettable, deep blue flowers are reason enough for the popularity of this easy to grow gentian. It should readily spread. ◐, E, 10 × 15cm/ 4 × 6in

***Viola soraria* 'Freckles'** Exquisite white violets, delicately freckled with lavender. Position at the front of the border, beneath shrubs or in containers. 10 × 30cm/4in × 1ft

◆ *Named violas do not, as a rule, come true from seed. They should be propagated by vegetative means in late summer or autumn.*

Libertia formosa Grassy foliage, of a good dark green, forms a basal clump to sprays of white flowers at the centre of which is a cluster of yellow stamens. Apart from a need for good drainage, libertia will flourish in either sun or part shade. Seedlings are often to be found around the parent plant. E, 90 × 60cm/3 × 2ft

Smilacina racemosa This is a plant to enliven a shady area. Creamy flower panicles are produced on arching stems above handsome foliage. At the season's end cut leaves back to ground level. An application of leaf mould in the spring will prove beneficial. ◐, 75 × 75cm/2½ × 2½ft

Trillium grandiflorum roseum Trilliums are amongst the most desirable of late spring plants but are, regrettably, slow to establish. They need humus rich, moist, well-drained, acidic, or at least

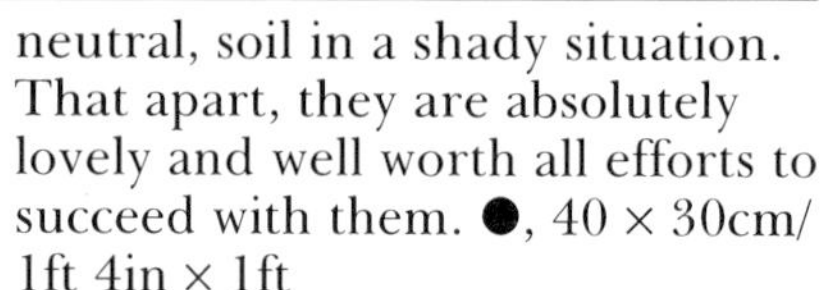

neutral, soil in a shady situation. That apart, they are absolutely lovely and well worth all efforts to succeed with them. ●, 40 × 30cm/ 1ft 4in × 1ft

Primula sieboldii Lightly fringed, unusually veined flowers which range in colour from pale blue, through white and pink to dark red are the principal features of this small primula which, by midsummer, will have died down completely. Plant in a cool, moist spot with a little shade. 15 × 15cm/6 × 6in

Dicentra spectabilis Bleeding heart is the name by which this perennial is widely known. Most likely this is on account of the rosy red flower which, in bud, dangles like a heart or locket from an arching stem. 60 × 45cm/2 × 1½ft

◆ *'Alba', a white form, is worth growing as well. Both are content in either a sunny place or a partly shaded one.*

Hesperis matronalis Strictly speaking a perennial, sweet rocket is short lived but may be relied upon to seed around freely. Seedlings vary from white to lilac, but all are scented, the fragrance most pronounced in the evening. Double flowered varieties may be grown but need to be propagated from cuttings. ◐, 75 × 60cm/2½ × 2ft

Thermopsis montana Often mistaken for a lupin flower, thermopsis makes a good border perennial but allow space for its running habit. 75 × 75cm/ $2^1/_2 \times 2^1/_2$ft

Mertensia virginica Cultivation of this unusual plant is not difficult although it needs good drainage. Later it will die down completely. ◐, 60 × 45cm/2 × $1^1/_2$ft

Limnanthes douglasii The poached egg plant is wonderfully sunny. Traditionally an annual, it will readily seed to come up each year. ❍, 15cm/6in

***Geum rivale* 'Leonard's Variety'** Although commonly known as water avens, geum will succeed in most ordinary garden soil and is unfussy about situation. In mild winters the foliage remains semi-evergreen. 45 × 45cm/$1^1/_2 \times 1^1/_2$ft

◆ G. rivale *'Lionel Cox' is a highly desirable hybrid of soft primrose with a hint of apricot.* G. rivale *'Album' is an equally attractive white form. All geums flower over a long period.*

Paeonia arietina Flowers of this free-growing plant vary from deep to light magenta-pink or, exceptionally, to pale rose-pink. Peonies appreciate humus-rich soil and will benefit from an annual dressing of well rotted manure or garden compost. They will continue to flourish in the same spot for a great many years without disturbance. 75 × 60cm/ 2½ × 2ft

Bulbs and Tubers

Late-flowering tulips, amongst them beautifully fringed parrots, elegantly shaded *viridiflora* and exciting paeony types, complement the herbaceous plants which are currently filling beds and borders. In addition, the first of the showy alliums, camassias and lily-of-the-valley underline the continuing importance of bulbous plants to the overall spring display.

The succession of colour and interest in the garden, to which bulbs make such a major contribution, does not, unfortunately, come about by accident. More than any other plantings, schemes involving bulbs need to be planned well in advance. From midsummer onwards bulbs are on offer for sale both in garden centres and through nursery catalogues; the earlier in the season, the wider the choice. Later, planting should be undertaken throughout the autumn to be completed by Christmas.

Going around the garden now, notebook in hand, is not such a bad idea. Gaps in borders, or even whole areas, which would benefit from extra plantings of bulbs may be noted, and sympathetic choices made whilst the effect to be aimed for is fresh in the mind.

Irises in May

Among the spring flowering irises are those known as Intermediate Bearded Irises. These originate from hybridizing the taller sorts with *I. chamaeiris* to produce a wide range of excitingly coloured, medium-height plants of around 30cm/2ft. Grown in full sun, and given well drained soil, they should flower freely and require little in the way of management. Overcrowded rhizomes may be lifted and divided after the flowering period is over.

Shown here are Californian hybrid irises. These grow to between 30 and 60cm/1–2ft and are coloured from deep purple to white.

Tulipa **'Noranda'** Blood-red petals, tinted orange at the edges, make a powerful border statement, interplanted with cream-coloured pansies. 45cm/1½ft

◆ *These fringed and lacerated tulips are both elegant and different. For early May, choose 'Blue Heron', 'Fringed Beauty' or 'Maja'. For later colour, pick 'Burgundy' or 'Fancy Frills'.*

Tulipa **'Black Parrot'** One of the most striking of all parrot tulips, here combined with the lime-green bracts of *Euphorbia amygdaloides* var. *robbiae*. 45cm/1½ft

Tulipa **'Spring Green'** Green shaded petals are the hallmark of the delicately coloured, superbly elegant *viridiflora* tulips. Underplant this variety with a white flowered dicentra for a cool, sophisticated look. 45cm/1½ft

◆ *Stronger mixes, each striped green, are to be found in the varieties 'Golden Artist', 'Hollywood' and 'Pimpernel'.*

Shown here are 'China Pink' tulips underplanted with forget-me-nots. Such a scheme amply illustrates the effectiveness of generous plantings which achieve their impact through a limited range of colour. The soft blue haze acts as a perfect foil to the satin-pink of the lily flowers, understated but of classical appeal.

Lily flowered tulips are not only a graceful addition to any spring border but are also excellent as cut flowers for indoor display.

***Allium aflatunense* 'Purple Sensation'** White lychnis and pink forget-me-nots provide a subtly coloured carpet for the striking heads of this cultivated form of onion. An arrangement like this one makes good use of annuals, bulbs and perennials. Display the long-lasting flowers in vases either fresh or dried. 1m/3ft

Hyacinthoides non-scriptus As a carpet in woodland dappled in spring sunlight the common bluebell must be without equal. In a garden bluebells should be restricted to less formal areas where they will quickly naturalize. 45 × 30cm/1½ × 1ft

Rhodohypoxis baurii Grow these truly miniature flowers in peaty soil dressed with horticultural grit to protect against winter wet. ❍, 5cm/2in

Camassia leichtlinii In the wild these hardy, bulbous plants are to be found in moist grasslands. Within a garden provide ample moisture during the growing season. Obtain bulbs in the autumn and plant to a depth of 5cm/2in to form clumps in a border which does not dry out. 75 × 30cm/2½ × 1ft

◆ *Camassias may be propagated from seed and should reach flowering sized bulbs within four years.*

Convallaria majalis A place for lily-of-the-valley should be found in every garden on account of the beautifully fragrant flowers. They are, in fact, totally unfussy and will succeed in the least promising of situations, often in quite dense shade. Provide them with a good start by planting in well composted soil, then allow to increase. ◐, ●, 20cm/8in

***Aesculus neglecta* 'Erythroblastos'**
This slow growing tree delights in the spring with new leaves of shrimp pink. In this respect it makes an excellent alternative to *Acer pseudoplatanus* 'Brilliantissimum'. ❍, 10 × 10m/ 33 × 33ft

SHRUBS AND TREES

As a shield against the weather, to mask a boundary, as structure to a border or, simply, as a specimen in the lawn, shrubs and trees are an essential component of all gardens from the tiniest to the largest.

Late spring sees them possibly at their best as new leaves unfurl and previously bare branches are ripe with blossom. Indeed, the spring flowering almonds, cherries and crabs are one of the chief delights of the season and their continued popularity is completely understandable.

Much enjoyment may be had by planning planting schemes to complement these flowering trees and shrubs. Neighbouring bulbs and perennials, even annuals, may be deliberately chosen to contrast with or reflect the same colour tones.

Where space is restricted, the majority of trees and shrubs will suffer no harm if judicious pruning takes place throughout the year to restrict growth.

***Malus × schiedeckeri* 'Red Jade'**
Later on the branches of this tree will be laden with deep red crab apples lasting well into winter. In spring it is a profusion of pink and white blossom. A weeping habit makes this most suitable for growing as a specimen in grass. 4 × 6m/13 × 20ft

◆ *For bright yellow fruits, and an otherwise similar habit although not weeping, grow* M. × zumi *'Golden Hornet'.*

***Sorbus aria* 'Lutescens'** Shimmering new leaves appear white felted, an effect caused by a white tomentum on the upper surfaces. As they develop throughout the summer, so the colour changes to grey-green. Whitebeams are hardy, of easy cultivation, suitable as windbreaks and tolerant of chalk. 10 × 10m/33 × 33ft

◆ *In this situation the sorbus is used both as a specimen and a focal point to break up an otherwise flat area of garden.*

***Prunus* 'Kanzan'** Although unfailing in popularity, its vibrancy may not be to everyone's taste and something a little softer, such as *P.* 'Hokusai' or *P.* 'Pink Perfection', may be preferred. For pure white, *P.* 'Tai Haku', the great white cherry, is near perfect. 8 × 8m/26 × 26ft

◆ *The majority of the trees and shrubs illustrated here may well, in a mild season, commence flowering in April.*

Cercis siliquastrum The Judas tree is smothered in small pea-like flowers in mid-spring followed by red pods later. It is deciduous, fully hardy but best planted in a sunny position, perhaps as a specimen or focal point in the garden. ❍, 10 × 10m/33 × 33ft

***Spiraea* 'Arguta'** Lovely arching stems wreathed in white give rise to the name bridal veil. This would make a graceful centrepiece to a white-themed bed. 2.4 × 2.4m/8 × 8ft

Choisya ternata The Mexican orange blossom will flower in spring and often again later in the year (see p. 214). E, 2 × 2m/ 6 × 6ft

Cytisus* × *kewensis A spreading broom for the rock garden or to fall over a low wall. Lightly trim after flowering. ○, 45cm × 1.5m/ 1½ × 5ft

***Exochorda* × *macrantha* 'The Bride'** Weeping stems bearing conspicuous paper-white flowers sweep downwards in late spring to form a compact, shapely mound. Pruning should take place immediately after flowering. 'The Bride' is unsuitable for growing on chalk; an alternative would be *E. koroikowii*. ○, 2.4 × 3m/8 × 10ft

◆ *When planting take note of ultimate height and spread. Shrubs such as this are spoilt if they become crowded and lose their shape and form.*

With all planting, consideration needs to be given to form. By mixing together plants which differ in leaf, habit, texture and, of course, flower a sense of monotony or sameness is avoided. Here the darkly flushed leaves of *Weigela florida* 'Foliis Purpureis' are balanced with the upright habit of *Syringa* 'Antoine Buchner' and the twiggy growth of *Cotoneaster horizontalis*. Both the weigela and lilac will flower around the same time whilst the cotoneaster will be bright with berry in autumn.

Clematis montana White flowers mark the true montana. Pink flowered varieties, often referred to as montana, are all named forms. All are capable of growing to several metres depending on soil, type and aspect.

***Clematis* 'Nelly Moser'** This accommodating clematis, with its cartwheel effect of mauve-lilac bars on the petals, remains unfailingly popular. Try it in a pot or through a shrub. ◐, 2.4m/8ft

◆ *Flowers, repeated in late summer and early autumn, will fade if planted in sun. Best on a west or east aspect.*

***Ceanothus* 'Blue Mound'** Ceanothus are amongst the loveliest of shrubs and most worthy of garden space. Sadly, not all are entirely hardy so a position affording some shelter needs to be found. 'Blue Mound' is spring-flowering; others will bloom later in the year. ❍, E, 1.5 × 2m/5 × 6ft

◆ *In a very cold area try* C. × thyrsiflorus *which is generally regarded to be one of the hardiest varieties.*

Halesia monticola Once established in its preferred situation the snowdrop tree will thrive. For this it requires full sun, moist, free-draining soil which is acid or neutral. ○, 6 × 4m/ 20 × 13ft

◆ *For a rose-coloured flower, rather than white, grow* H. monticola *'Rosea'.*

Convolvulus cneorum Silky, silvery leaves set off the appealing pinky-white flowers. This shrub is tender and needs a sheltered, well drained, sunny spot. ○, E, 1 × 1.2m/3 × 4ft

Paeonia delavayi var. ***ludlowii*** All the tree peonies are handsome shrubs which fit in well into the mixed border. 2.4 × 2.4m/8 × 8ft

***Paeonia suffruticosa* 'Situfukujin'** Named forms of the 'Moutan Paeony' are widely available. Most are semi-double or double in shades of pink, red and white. 2.4 × 2.4m/8 × 8ft

For those with acidic soil the growing of rhododendrons presents no problems. Perhaps more than any other shrub they are ideal subjects to form a backdrop to a border, garden or even landscape. Banks of rhododendrons belong, very naturally, to the large-scale garden or park, but smaller varieties will sit quite comfortably in a more domestic setting. Illustrated above are two of the more compact types, 'Golden Torch' and 'Sneezy'.

***Rhododendron* Azalea 'Hino-mayo'** Recommended as a free flowering, compact form, 'Hino-mayo' would make a container grown plant. E, 1.5 × 1.5m/5 × 5ft

◆ *Plants grown in pots must be kept well watered during dry periods and afforded some shade in the day.*

***Rhododendron* Hybrid 'Blue Star'** These violet blue flowers are a pleasing contrast to the more widely grown pinks and yellows. E, 1.5 × 1.5m/5 × 5ft

May represents the main flowering period of rhododenrons (and azaleas) and those gardens which specialize in their cultivation are possibly seen at their best during this month. Those shown here are some of the smaller ones which will lend themselves to the majority of garden situations. Top left is the dwarf, evergreen Hybrid 'Peeping Tom' whilst on the right is Azalea 'Palestrina', a white flowered evergreen growing to 1.2m/4ft. Bottom right is *R. yakushimanum* whose pink flowers fade to white and which will reach 1.5m/5ft. On the left is a flower stem of *R.* Azalea 'Hino-mayo', height 1.5m/5ft. Pictured in the centre is the evergreen Hybrid 'Elizabeth', eventually reaching 1.2m/4ft.

***Rosa* 'Frühlingsgold'** Long-reaching stems are weighed down with semi-double, butter-yellow, fragrantly scented flowers at this time of the year. 2.2 × 2m/7 × 6ft

***Rosa rugosa* 'Alba'** This vigorous rose is seldom without flower throughout the summer months. It is suitable for hedging. 2 × 2m/6 × 6ft

***Rosa xanthina* 'Canary Bird'** The first roses of summer are something rather special, to be anticipated with intense pleasure. 'Canary Bird' is amongst the earliest to flower and its cheerful canary-yellow blooms above fresh, ferny foliage are especially welcome. Once the first crop of flowers is over, late summer will produce a second flush. 2.2 × 2.2m/7 × 7ft

Rosa hugonis Soft, primrose-yellow flowers are arranged along gracefully arching branches on this early-flowering rose. 2.2 × 2m/7 × 6ft

Fremontodendron mexicanum Fremontodendron is best trained as a wall shrub where it will rapidly cover its allotted space. ❍, E, 6m/20ft

Genista lydia Golden flowers completely cover this rounded shrub during the late spring and early summer. Compact in habit. 60 × 60cm/2 × 2ft

Fothergilla major Scented white flowers appear before the leaves. In autumn foliage turns a rich red. Best in moist acid soil. 3 × 3m/10 × 10ft

Few would deny the magnificence of a laburnum tunnel on this scale. Not only does it provide visual interest but it also serves the purpose of creating welcome shade during the hot days of summer.

***Laburnum* × *watereri* 'Vossii'** (*right*) may be grown as a specimen tree when its splendid flower racemes may be enjoyed each May. A word of caution – all parts of the laburnum are poisonous. 10 × 10m/33 × 33ft

Wisteria floribunda A well-grown wisteria will almost certainly excite interest. Observed in winter, the gnarled wood of a mature specimen is particularly appealing, whilst in early summer the long, flower racemes over fresh green foliage are utterly beautiful. ❍, 9m/30ft

◆ *A curtain of white will be achieved by growing* W. floribunda *'Alba'. For scent, look to the sinensis forms. Pruning is usually carried out twice a year. In summer, prune long side-growth back to four or five leaves. In winter, shorten back to two buds.*

The Water Garden

It is generally agreed that one of the most difficult aspects of maintaining a pond is keeping the water clear. All too often the surface is taken over with blanket weed, or similar, and what was once sparkling water is reduced to disappointing murkiness.

Oxygenating plants, either floating or submerged, will go some way towards resolving the problem and, whilst not especially decorative, will aid a return to more healthy conditions.

Fish, too, serve a practical as well as decorative purpose. The introduction of goldfish, common carp, rudd and roach will assist in the control of insect pests to be found in and around the pond.

Encouraging wildlife, in the form of frogs, toads, newts and dragonflies, is yet another way in which a natural balance may be sustained and problems minimized, if not eliminated.

Aponogeton distachyos Water hawthorn bears white flowers with black centres. Planted up to a depth of 45cm/1½ft it should help to keep water clear.

Myriophyllum aquaticum Parrot's feather flourishes just beneath the surface of the water.

Orontium aquaticum Apart from its oxygenating properties, this is an attractive plant in its own right. Unusual, and rather strange, poker-like flowers, themselves tipped yellow, rise out of green sheafed leaves. The whole plant should be placed in 30cm/1ft of water.

Felicia amelloides Blue marguerites look positively splendid in pots, particularly when grouped together as here. Felicia is not hardy and so pots should not be placed outdoors until all frosts are past.
45 × 30cm/1½ × 1ft

Planting Pots for Summer

Summer is a time for colour, for exuberant plantings, for showy effects. Terraces, sitting out areas, patios and pathways may all be brought alive with pots and containers massed to the brim with exciting, lively summer displays. Now is the time to start filling all manner of containers in preparation for the months to come. It matters little what is used, providing allowance is made for drainage. The secret of success is to be generous with plant material, filling to capacity to create wonderful, burgeoning results. Always allow, however, room for roots to expand but not too much as this will leave areas of earth which will simply go 'stale'. The compost, or growing medium, should be suited to the plant, perhaps lime-free as in the case of lime-hating plants, and it pays to cover the surface of the pot when planted with a layer of horticultural grit; this will look smarter, help conserve moisture and minimize disturbance of the soil when watering.

Aeonium arboreum Brought outside for the summer months, the tender aeonium contributes both style and variety to this thoughtfully planned gravel garden. The purple-leafed form, *A. arboreum* 'Atropurpureum' would look equally striking.

Abutilon megapotamicum Although not completely hardy, this abutilon is a lovely subject for a container.

A simple handcart utilized as a plant container. The effect is visually stunning. By limiting the material to white marguerites, pink pelargoniums and trailing lobelia a sense of unity and purpose is achieved. Siting containers is important – a plain background eliminates all distractions.

Hanging baskets form a traditional part of summer displays. Line the basket either with moss or, as here, a polythene sheet into which holes are cut in the sides. Fill with compost, water retentive granules and a fertilizing agent.

Plant up the basket, tucking plants into the holes made in the sides. Firm plants and water throroughly. Set aside in a sheltered place for plants to establish and develop. Keep watered.

The completed basket is ready for hanging out. Avoid a windy situation and ensure that fixings are strong enough to carry the weight.

Baskets dry out very easily. Water daily, twice daily in hot weather. As the summer progresses, apply a nitrogen feed to keep the basket looking good into autumn.

***Fuchsia* 'Red Spider'** Pendulous fuchsias are ideal to be included in hanging baskets or containers. They mix well with other plants or may be considered on their own. 'Red Spider' has long crimson sepals and rose-pink corolla.

***Fuchsia* 'Mrs. Churchill'** Although it is inclined to be reluctant to branch out, this fuchsia has been used on its own most successfully in a hanging pot. The result is simple, unfussy yet charming.

Clashing colours combine in this window box to make a startling but spirited display. Petunias of shocking pink are mixed with red pelargoniums, orange nemesia and blue and white lobelia. Overall success lies in the quantity and quality of the plant material.

A colourful arrangement of begonias mixed with mauve flowered pelargoniums is the mainstay of this window box. In addition to flower colour, the begonias add a sense of luxuriance with their shapely, glossy leaves. These further serve to quieten the scheme.

STAKING
Successful border management depends on effective staking if tall growing perennials are to keep their shape and withstand the vagaries of the weather. Choose from manufactured supports, canes and twine or old fashioned pea sticks.

Staking now, before the growth of summer, will ensure that problems do not arise later on. Here the tall-growing cardoon, *Cynara cardunculus*, is supported with bamboo canes and string.

Hardy Biennials
Seed of hardy biennials like forget-me-nots, foxgloves (shown on the right), honesty, sweet williams and wallflowers should be sown in prepared seed drills this month. By autumn they should be of sufficient size to transplant into beds and borders where they are to flower.

Alternatively, as with hardy annuals, they may be sown directly into the positions where they will flower and any excess plants can then be thinned out. If the thinning out is done carefully, without disturbance to the remaining plants, this can result in stronger plants in the bed with a better display of flowers. If a biennial produces a flower bud in its first year it is best to pinch it out as the subsequent and main flowering season will be the poorer.

Half-hardy annuals
Half-hardy annuals, sown in March (see page 39), should now be ready for planting out into final flowering positions for summer displays. Naturally this should be delayed if there is any risk of frost.

Dahlias
Dahlia tubers, overwintered in a frost free environment, may now be set out.

Tubers should be planted about 1m/3ft apart to correspond with the growth of individual plants. They should remain in situ until the first frosts of autumn.

Dahlias prefer medium to heavy garden soil in sun.

SUMMER BEDDING

Glorious displays in the months ahead owe their success, in part, to preparation and planning taking place now. Hardy annuals, sown in position in April, should be starting to get away and to these may be added half-hardy ones.

Where it has not been possible to raise suitable plants at home, garden centres and nurseries will have a good selection of bedding plants at this time from which to choose.

Bedding schemes may be strictly colour themed or mixed, depending on personal taste and requirements. Whatever, it is important to keep new plants well watered to encourage root growth.

Tagetes patula French marigolds remain a popular choice for bedding. A less conventional use would be to edge a vegetable plot with them. ❍, 30 × 30cm/1 × 1ft

Salvia splendens Trail a blaze of colour through any border with the scarlet blooms of this bedding salvia. Delay planting until there is no risk of frost. ❍, 30 × 30cm/ 1 × 1ft

***Gazania* 'Dorothy'** A bright daisy-type flower which should be given an open, sunny position. Gazania flowers close up when out of the sun and in the evening. ❍, 20 × 20cm/8 × 8in

KITCHEN GARDEN
Work begun last month in the kitchen garden continues in this. To the main crops sown previously may be added Brussels sprouts, cauliflower, courgette (zucchini), cucumber, endive, fennel, peppers, runner beans and sweetcorn (maize). Seeds which have come through, thin where necessary. This particularly applies to root crops.

Seed drills may be lightly hoed, and certainly between rows, once seedlings have developed. Attention to this aspect of vegetable growing will pay off in the future.

If it has not been possible to grow from seed, young vegetable plants may be bought now from garden centres.

CLIP HEDGES
Although the main hedge cutting period takes place in late summer, quick-growing or ornamental hedges, such as box, may be trimmed in the late spring to retain their shape. Use a guide line to ensure that tops are straight and level.

CHECK LIST

- Maintain a programme of weeding (p.62).
- Plant perennials for maximum effect (p.66).
- Note gaps to be filled with bulbs for next year (p.71).
- Control algae on ponds (p.89).
- Plant up pots for summer colour (p.90).
- Fill hanging baskets (p.92).
- Stake tall-growing perennials (p.94).
- Sow seed of hardy biennials (p.95).
- Plant out half hardy annuals (p.95).
- Set out dahlia tubers (p.95).
- Complete summer bedding (p.96).
- Continue sowing of vegetable seeds. Thin root crops (p.97).
- Trim ornamental hedges (p.97).
- Keep pests and diseases under control. Spray against greenfly and rose blackspot. Renew slug pellets.

STRAW STRAWBERRIES
Just before the flowers of the strawberry plants open, hoe the ground thoroughly and then cover with fairly short straw to prevent the fruit from being splashed with mud. If late frosts occur, pull the straw over the blooms to protect them.

JUNE

WITH THE ONSET OF JUNE, spring slips quietly away and summer, the glory of the garden, gathers pace. This is the month of wonderfully fragrant roses, of cascading clematis, and of borders over-spilling with favourite flowers – campanulas, delphiniums, dianthus, irises, oriental poppies and sweetly smelling violas.

Hard work undertaken in the preceding weeks should now pay off. Vigilance in the past where weeds are concerned should mean fewer seedlings taking hold. Developing plants reduce the problem further. By June staking should be in place and errant climbers tied in firmly to supports.

Tasks are no longer onerous, rather routine. Constant dead heading, a pleasure on a warm evening, seldom a chore, results not only in well manicured borders but assists in prolonging the flowering period. Lawns mown regularly, and edges trimmed, present a crisp background to floral displays. Spring-flowering perennials cut to the ground will very quickly throw up a mound of fresh, new foliage, possibly a bonus flower or two.

***Geranium endressii* 'Wargrave Pink'** All of the hardy geraniums, or cranesbills, flower over many weeks and the pretty foliage forms a good ground cover. 60 × 60cm/2 × 2ft

◆ *Plant hardy geraniums around the base of shrub roses where their soft colours will complete a decorative picture.*

Geranium sanguineum* var. *striatum Pale pink flowers like these tone with so many herbaceous perennials, seldom looking out of place. ❍, 30 × 45cm/1 × 1½ft

Generously stocked borders, as this one, are designed for impact and to provide a continuous flower display over several months. In the foreground liberal plantings of pink dicentra, flowering from May, spill out onto the path to mask an otherwise straight edge. Complementing these is a ribbon of *Gladiolus byzantinus*, the daring colour of which purposely draws the eye along and picks up the tones of the hardy geranium. Mauve nepeta, planted at intervals, acts as a foil to predominantly pink shades. Towards the back the first oriental poppies are bursting bud whilst self-sown foxgloves jostle among great clumps of delphiniums, yet to flower, and thalictrum.

Throughout, attention is paid to detail. Different leaf form, controlled use of colour, varying heights, plentiful plant material, all contribute to the overall sense of harmony. Even care has been taken to construct the path of stone material similar to that of the boundary wall.

Scabiosa caucasica Scabious, with their fine, papery petals, thrive on any fertile soil in a sunny position. Dead head regularly to induce repeat flowering. ❍, 60 × 60cm/2 × 2ft

Summery aquilegia in shades of pink and violet-blue happily mix here with rose-coloured silene and aromatic nepeta. Combining similar tones results in a sympathetic, harmonious whole.

◆ *Although the effect is of a random, cottage garden, colour and plant types are in fact firmly restricted and managed.*

In this border flag irises are partnered with gladiolus, peonies and hardy geraniums. To succeed, the iris should be planted in a position where their rhizomes receive full sun. Every three or so years, following flowering, lift plants and divide overcrowded rhizomes. Discard tired middles, cut new pieces from the outer edges and replant in rejuvenated soil. Reduce leaves by about two thirds. Iris lend themselves to cultivation in a bed to themselves. Leaves growing in fan shapes remain attractive after the flowers.

Primula helodoxa The strong colour of this species primula picks up the tone of the yellow flag, *Iris pseudacorus*, in the background. 60 × 45cm/2 × 1ft

◆ *Planting around this pond is without compromise. Clumps are lavish and sited with confidence.*

Alchemilla mollis The lady's mantle is surely without equal as a foil to other plantings. Sprays of lime flowers over grey-green leaves. 60 × 60cm/ 2 × 2ft

Lupinus polyphyllus Easily raised from seed, lupins are amongst the brightest of June flowers and are available in a wide range of colours, including many named forms. In a mixed border plant behind later perennials to avoid gaps once the flowering period is over.

Because lupins are not long lived plants, those which have lost their vigour are best replaced from time to time with young, fresh stock.

***Dianthus* 'Pike's Pink'** Border pinks begin their long flowering period in June. This delightful variety is one of many suitable for the rock garden or for edging a path. All require good drainage and an open, sunny situation. ○, E, 15 × 15cm/ 6 × 6in

A low wall like this may be planted up to provide a tapestry of colour from springtime into summer. Although the purple aubrieta is now virtually over, awaiting shearing back, the cheerful yellow *Corydalis lutea*, seen on the left, will continue to flower for many weeks to come. Corydalis may be left to seed and can be relied upon to gain a foothold in the most impossible of cracks and crevices.

Centranthus ruber Commonly known as valerian, centranthus flowers in shades of pink, red and white and is a prolific self seeder. Notwithstanding, it should be welcome for the ways in which it will find a home where little else will grow. 1m × 45cm/3 × 1½ft

Enjoying the free draining site is the helianthemum, rock rose. This small spreading shrub is to be found in a wide range of colour and is in bloom from late spring onwards.

Variegated London pride, *Saxifraga* 'Aureopunctata', forms fleshy, evergreen rosettes which contrast here with tiny ferns seeded into shadier, damper spots.

***Paeonia officinalis* 'Rubra Plena'** Cottage gardens of the past would all, as a matter of course, have included this double peony, in cultivation since the sixteenth century. Peonies can commence flowering as early as April. 60 × 60cm/2 × 2ft

Papaver orientale Red is the traditional colour of oriental poppies but gorgeous shades of pink, white and orange appear in named hybrids. 1m × 60cm/3 × 2ft

***Penstemon* 'Red Knight'** Tubular flowers of the hardier hybrids appear continuously from June until October, later in mild weather. ○, E, 75 × 45cm/2½ × 1½ft

◆ *Delay cutting plants back to ground level until the spring. Old foliage and flower stems will provide greater protection against cold.*

***Helianthemum* 'Supreme'** To keep the rock roses in good shape they should be cut back fairly severely once the flowering period is over. To neglect this will result in straggly plants which become very woody. Helianthemums may be propagated from semi-ripe cuttings taken in late summer. ○, E, 15 × 45cm/6in × 1½ft

Lychnis chalcedonica Startling red flowers, true vermillion and somewhat difficult to place, appear from early summer and look best massed together. Maltese cross, dating from the time of the crusades, enjoys a sunny place in the garden and will stand up better with some support if wind is a problem. 1m × 45cm/3 × 1½ft

◆ *Look out for the rare, double red as well as pink and white forms.*

This soft, alluring summer scheme relies on two principal players. In the foreground are the spherical, purple heads of the ornamental onion, *Allium aflatunense* (1.2m × 30cm/4 × 1ft), whilst further back are ethereal spikes of *Asphodelus albus* (1m × 30cm/3 × 1ft). By interplanting with blue and white agapanthus the effect could be sustained later into the season.

Both plants, as well as agapanthus, need to be grown in a sunny, well drained border.

Stachys macrantha These purplish-pink flowers belong to a hardy herbaceous perennial with dark leaves carried on erect stems. 45 × 45cm/1½ × 1½ft

◆ Stachys macrantha *is a good choice to grow with old shrub roses of similar hues.*

Baptisia australis An unusual and lovely plant with its indigo-blue flowers and blue-green foliage. 75 × 60cm/2½ × 2ft

Iris missouriensis Damp soil is a requirement of this handsome lavender-blue iris. For this reason a bog garden or the margins of a pond would provide the correct environment for generous clumps like these. 60 × 60cm/2 × 2ft

◆ *With particular schemes in mind, it is best to make initial purchases of plants when they are in flower so that exact colour tints are known.*

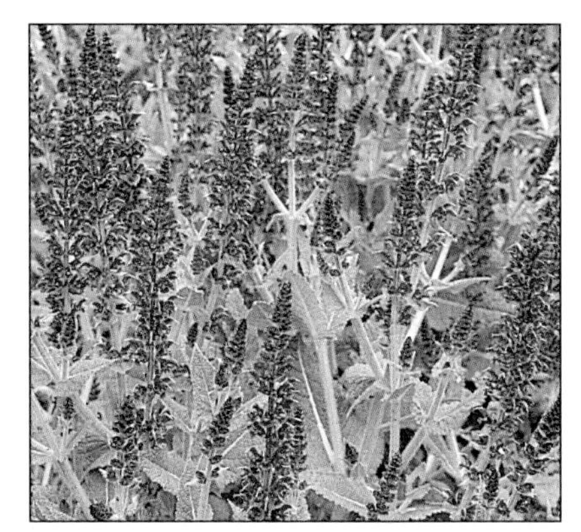

***Salvia* × *superba* 'Mainacht'** A good front-of-border plant. An exciting combination would be achieved by pairing it with deep orange poppies. 60 × 30cm/ 2 × 1ft

Polemonium reptans Jacob's ladder, to be found seeding in all old gardens, is, like aquilegia, useful as a filler in a mixed border. 30 × 45cm/1 × 1½ft

◆ *For something a little special, grow* P. foliosissimum *with lovely, pale lilac cups lit by orange stamens.*

***Geranium pratense* 'Mrs Kendall Clark'** This attractive pale form of the meadow cranesbill will form useful clumps at the front of the border. 75m × 45cm/ 2½ × 1½ft

◆ *Geraniums are invaluable plants in the herbaceous border, perfect companions for roses and other flowering shrubs.*

Lilium martagon Turk's cap lilies in white, pink and maroon are wonderful when allowed to naturalize in grass. ◐, 1.5m × 30cm/5 × 1ft

Gillenia trifoliata Flights of graceful white flowers float over sparsely leaved, red stems on this unusual and sought after herbaceous perennial. 1m × 60cm/3 × 2ft

◆ *Gillenia would look particularly charming rising from a carpet of the little white violet,* Viola cornuta alba.

Imagine this border scheme in the twilight with the ethereal beauty of all these whites made so much more intense by the gathering darkness. Holding centre stage is the lovely, single peony, 'White Wings', supported by white aquilegias, foxgloves, some a soft apricot, foaming sprays of *Crambe cordifolia* and nodding heads of *Viola cornuta alba.*

Combinations such as this one are within everyone's reach. They require no more than careful and thoughtful planning, patience, imagination and, above all, commitment and resolve.

Asphodeline lutea From grassy foliage rise tall, spiky stems carrying straw yellow flowers set among hide-coloured bracts. 1m × 60cm/3 × 2ft

◆ *Slightly later, and a rather paler yellow, is* A. liburnica. *Neither is difficult to cultivate.*

Cephalaria gigantea Soft primrose yellow flowers on this tall-growing relative of scabious. This is a splendid border plant. 2 × 1.2m/6 × 4ft

Centaurea macrocephala Do not be put off by the rather coarse leaves of this border knapweed. The rich buttery flowers surrounded by brown parchment bracts make a bold and sunny statement and are marvellous to dry. To extend the scheme of yellow, plant *C. macrocephala* alongside the new English rose, 'Graham Thomas'. 1m × 60cm/3 × 2ft

◆ *Include in the June border the smaller growing, deep blue* C. montana, *the mountain knapweed.*

***Campanula latiloba* 'Hidcote Amethyst'** Drifts of this beautifully coloured campanula would enhance any border scheme. Divide every three or so years to maintain virile, healthy plants. 1.2m × 30cm/4 × 1ft

Hosta sieboldiana Grow hostas for their bold, dramatic foliage; their flowers are, in comparison, less significant. This one has strong glaucous leaves and will do anywhere where the soil does not dry out completely. Beware of slugs eating the leaves. ◐, 75 × 75cm/2½ × 2½ft

Delphiniums No June border should be without these tall-growing, floriferous herbaceous perennials available in a wide range of colours. 1.5m × 60cm/ 5 × 2ft

◆ *Delphiniums usually require some form of support to prevent stems becoming damaged by wind and rain.*

'Marguerite Hilling' Warm-pink blooms run the length of attractively arching stems on a mature bush of this hybrid species rose. 2.4 × 2.2m/8 × 7ft

'Pink Bells' A very pretty ground-cover rose for a sunny bank. Sprays of pink pompon flowers are carried above glossy foliage over a long period. 60cm × 1.2m/2 × 4ft

'Ballerina' Of all the dwarf polyantha roses, 'Ballerina' is amongst the best known. A free flowering shrub which may be grown in the border, in a pot or trained as a half-standard. 1.2 × 1m/4 × 3ft

'Buff Beauty' Hybrid musk roses are noted for the fragrance of their flowers and this one is no exception. Warm apricot blooms, fully double, are carried in plentiful trusses at this time of year. 'Buff Beauty' could be trained to climb a trellis or pergola.
1.5 × 1.5m/5 × 5ft

'Gertrude Jekyll' One of many English roses which may be relied upon for their robust habit, abundance of flowers and disease free foliage. Reduce stems by about a half in late autumn or early winter to reduce the possibility of damage through wind rock.
1.2 × 1m/4 × 3ft

MODERN SHRUB ROSES

Sensuous roses confirm the presence of early summer. Their exquisite fragrance and the brilliance of their blooms evoke a magical atmosphere which is both intoxicating and romantic. The modern shrub rose, a comparatively recent introduction, contributes scent, form and colour and includes many which, in a short space of time, have rapidly established themselves as firm favourites and which are, happily, widely grown.

This arrangement of *Rosa* 'Mary Rose', hardy geraniums and scented violas illustrates one of the ways in which the modern shrub roses may be easily incorporated into a garden scheme.

'Tuscany Superb' Wonderful, velvety semi-double blooms of an intense dark crimson-maroon. Gallica roses often spread to form a substantial thicket. 1.5 × 1m/ 5 × 3ft

OLD SHRUB ROSES

Gallica, Damask, Alba, Centifolia and Moss, such names conjure up a real spirit of the past, of the Medes and the Persians, of the Crusaders and the Romans, of the dark and mysterious Middle Ages. For these are the roses of history, of forgotten centuries, the forerunners of today's garden shrubs.

Richly scented, magnificent blooms typify these lovely lax shrubs which convey to any garden a feeling for the antique, an air of maturity and a reassuring sense of permanency.

'Madame Zoetmans' Pale, blush-pink flowers of this compact shrub are buttoned green at the centre. Damask roses were originally cultivated for the production of attar, rose oil. 1.2 × 1m/4 × 3ft

◆ *Among the Damask roses are the romantically named 'Celsiana', 'Gloire de Guilan', 'Ispahan' and 'Kazanlük'. The flesh-pink buds of 'Madame Hardy' open to pure white.*

'Variegata di Bologna' Fully cupped, deliciously scented blooms are a hallmark of all the Bourbon roses some of which are striped. 1.5 × 1.2m/5 × 4ft

◆ *Included among the Bourbon roses are 'Madame Pierre Oger', 'Reine Victoria' and 'Souvenir de la Malmaison'.*

'Madame Isaac Pereire' Of all the Bourbon roses this must surely rank among the loveliest. Deeply cupped and quartered flowers are carried above vigorous, dark-green foliage. 2 × 1.5m/6 × 5ft

◆ *When pruning any shrub rose, aim for a nicely open framework by removing all congested growth from the centre of the bush.*

'Comte de Chambord' One of the Autumn Damask Roses, so called on account of their extended flowering season. 1.2 × 1m/4 × 3ft

***Rosa* 'Mundi'** (*Rosa gallica versicolor*) Blooms are unevenly striped rose-pink with cerise-pink. They are heavily scented. 1.2 × 1.2m/4 × 4ft

◆ *Grow* Rosa *'Mundi' as a low, compact hedge to divide one part of the garden or a flower border from another.*

Coppery tints of *R.* 'Edith Holden', partnered here with the pink and buff of *R.* 'Iced Ginger', hold together this modern planting scheme. In the background *Iris* 'Perryhill' is teamed with the scarlet bells of *Penstemon barbatus*. *Ophiopogon planiscapus* 'Nigrescens', a low growing, black-leafed grass, edges the front of the border.

MODERN BUSH ROSES

For sheer brilliance of bloom, for innovative colour, for massed display, the modern bush rose will satisfy all such demands and more besides. Included in this group are the Hybrid Teas, the most popular of all garden roses, multi-flowered Floribundas, and an extensive range of Miniature and Patio roses, many ideal for small gardens or pots. Among these will be found long-time favourites, such as 'Peace' and 'Super Star', as well as more recent introductions like 'Dame Wendy' or 'Savoy Hotel'.

'Royal William' Vigorous growth is matched with a succession of fragrant, velvety-crimson blooms of classic appearance. 1 × 1m/ 3 × 3ft

'Sweet Dream' Bushy, upright growth and dense foliage make this apricot-peach, patio rose suitable for the rock garden or for pot cultivation. 45cm/1½ft

◆ *All the Miniature and Patio roses are suitable for today's smaller gardens and are reliably hardy.*

'Iceberg' Of all the Floribundas 'Iceberg' is probably not only best known but most widely grown. It flowers over a long period, often well into winter. 1.2 × 1.2m/ 4 × 4ft

'Queen Elizabeth' An exceptionally vigorous, strongly growing rose which should be placed at the back of the border. 1.5 × 1m/5 × 3ft

'Madame Alfred Carrière' A vigorous Noisette climber bearing clusters of large double, fragrant flowers. It will tolerate partial shade. 3.5 × 3m/12 × 10ft

CLIMBING ROSES

Cascading from mature trees, draping arches and pergolas or clothing ancient walls, even covering an unsightly shed, the Climbing and Rambler roses may be put to endless use. Combine them with a complementary clematis for an eye-catching display of colour and interest over the summer period. Choose from soft, pastel shades, vibrant reds, oranges and yellows or cooling creams and whites.

From the past come much-loved 'Climbing Cécile Brunner', 'Gloire de Dijon' and 'Zéphirine Drouhin' whilst among the more modern are 'Compassion', 'Danse du Feu' and 'Schoolgirl'.

'Blush Noisette' An absolutely enchanting rose. This is the original Noisette producing a continuous display of semi-double, pink-white flowers, flushed with lilac, from summer until autumn. As a bonus the blooms are deliciously scented, smelling of cloves. 2.2m/7ft

◆ *Of all climbing roses, 'Blush Noisette' has the advantage of contained growth making it suitable for a variety of situations and particularly appropriate to the small garden. Of similar habit are the silky lemon 'Céline Forestier', modern coral-pink 'Dreamgirl', crimson 'Gruss an Teplitz' and bronze-yellow 'Maigold'.*

'Paul's Himalayan Musk' Surely one of the most beautiful of ramblers. Trailing growth carries sprays of tiny, blush-pink rosettes, each of which is borne on a thin stem. 9m/30ft

'New Dawn' Vigorous, fragrant and tolerant of some shade, partner this pale pink rose with the deep purple *Clematis viticella* 'Etoile Violette'. 3.5m/12ft

'Albéric Barbier' Starting out in bud a soft yellow, the double flowers of this sturdy, strong-growing rambler open a pleasing creamy white. 6m/20ft

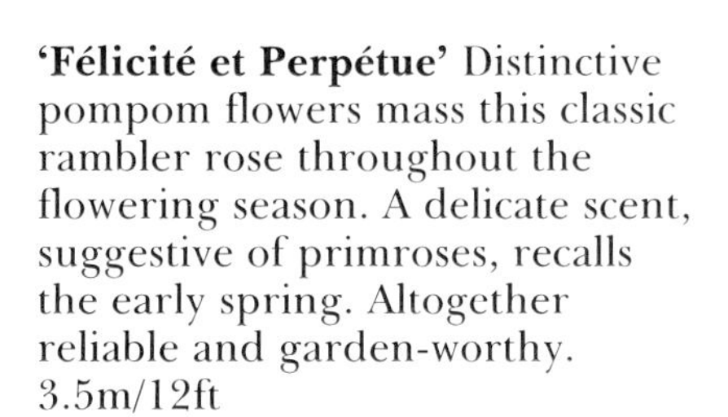

'Félicité et Perpétue' Distinctive pompom flowers mass this classic rambler rose throughout the flowering season. A delicate scent, suggestive of primroses, recalls the early spring. Altogether reliable and garden-worthy. 3.5m/12ft

CLIMBING AND RAMBLER ROSES
Some confusion arises over the terms climbing and rambler. Essentially the difference is simple. Climbing roses possess larger flowers than those to be found on ramblers, more closely resembling those of other garden roses. Generally they are likely to repeat their flowering whereas the ramblers flower mainly once only. The stems of climbing roses are stiff and are generally retained as a framework whilst ramblers have lax stems; those which have borne flowers are cut back to ground level after flowering (see August, page 185).

'Empress Josephine' A truly magnificent old French rose which will be in flower towards the end of June and early July, a period when the garden is really dominated by roses. 'Empress Josephine' has little scent but makes up for this failing with the number of its blooms in wonderful shades of pink. 1.2 × 1.2m/4 × 4ft

SHRUBS IN JUNE

June brings with it a succession of flowering shrubs many of which, like the mock oranges, lilacs and lavenders, are wonderfully scented and whose fragrance will flood the garden on a warm, summer's evening.

Climbers continue to contribute a well furnished look to the garden and in early summer there is no shortage of richly coloured clematis, delicate solanums, exotic passion flowers and sweet smelling honeysuckles from which to make a choice. Remember too the evergreen ivies, many lustrous with brightly variegated foliage.

Allow climbers to grow up and through traditional supports but also experiment with training them across the surface of the ground, along the top of walls and fences or to twine around posts as coloured standards.

***Solanum crispum* 'Glasnevin'** In a mild garden this wall-trained shrub will climb to 6m/20ft or more. Unfortunately it is only hardy to around –5C/23F so siting it in a really sheltered spot is of paramount importance. ❍, E or semi-E, 6m/20ft

***Clematis* 'Ernest Markham'** This is a strong growing clematis which will smother a wall with its vivid blooms. Best in full sun. 4m/12ft

◆ *Advice on pruning clematis is given on page 26.*

***Clematis* 'Niobe'** Display these velvety, ruby-red flowers against a variegated shrub, such as an aucuba, elaeagnus or holly, to show them off to effect. Niobe will succeed in most situations and will flower on and off for the greater part of the summer. 3m/10ft

Lavandula stoechas Use lavenders to line a path, edge a border, as a low hedge, within a herb garden, or simply for fragrant colour in a mixed bed. E, 1 × 1m/3 × 3ft

◆ *To prevent plants from becoming woody, clip hard back in the springtime.*

(*Opposite*) Silver leafed perennials act as a foil to the papery white flowers of the sprawling cistus which, in turn, is highlighted against a haze of blue ceanothus. This is a refreshingly cool scheme to counteract the hot days of summer. The cistus, planted in full sun and given sharp drainage, will delight for weeks to come with new flower buds opening day after day. Beds or borders, or parts of, planted in a similar manner are, importantly, restful in their own right. They give the eye, and spirit, a chance to relax, to have respite from an otherwise highly colourful, highly charged garden scene.

× **_Halimiocistus_** Given a hot, dry situation this charming little shrub will reward with a profusion of flowers from the late spring well into summer. In the early part of the year, remove straggly or damaged branches but avoid cutting into old wood. E, 60cm × 1.2m/2 × 4ft

Cornus kousa Small, rather delicate cream flowers are followed in the autumn by most unusual, strawberry-like fruits. Known as the Chinese dogwood. 3.6 × 4m/12 × 13ft

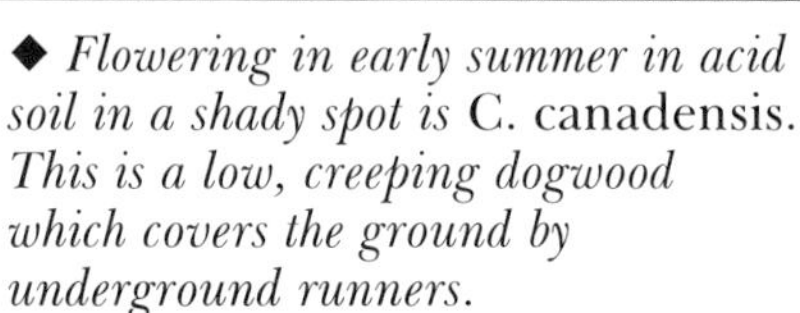

◆ *Flowering in early summer in acid soil in a shady spot is* C. canadensis. *This is a low, creeping dogwood which covers the ground by underground runners.*

Hydrangea anomala subsp. ***petiolaris*** Greenish-white, flat headed flowers held in large clusters will cover a mature plant of this self-clinging hydrangea in June. Once established this is a vigorous climber and is an excellent choice to grow against walls or up into trees. However, young plants are slow to put on growth, sometimes showing little appreciable development for a year or two. 8 × 1m/26 × 3ft

Cistus × hybridus Sun and good drainage are essential if this low growing shrub is to reward with a succession of flowers over a long period. Flower buds are tinted crimson before opening white. Equally hardy for a similar situation is the pale-pink flowered form, *C.* 'Silver Pink'. ❍, E, 1 × 1m/3 × 3ft

Abutilon* × *suntense This deciduous shrub will have been in flower from April in a warm, sunny situation. It develops tall, arching stems and, although it is frost hardy, it is best grown against a wall where it is possible to tie in any lax stems. Prune hard previous season's growth in early spring. ❍, 5 × 3m/15 × 10ft

***Philadelphus* 'Belle Etoile'** Mock oranges are beautifully scented shrubs for the June border. 'Belle Etoile' is one of the best. ❍, 2.4 × 2.4m/8 × 8ft

◆ *Where space is limited, grow one of the smaller varieties such as 'Sybille' or one of the doubles like 'Bouquet Blanc' or 'Coupe d'Argent'.*

***Clematis* 'Marie Boisselot'** Synonymous with *C.* 'Madame le Coultre', this elegant, white-flowered clematis should be found a place in every garden. In principle this climber only requires an annual light trim. Should it exceed its allotted space, or become tangled, cut back to ground level in spring. 3.5m/7½ft

***Kalmia latifolia* 'Nimuck Red Bud'** For those who garden on anything other than acidic or, at worst, neutral soil, the cultivation of *Kalmia* will prove an unequal struggle. Given the right conditions, the calico bush is a splendid, evergreen shrub producing conspicuous open flowers from spring into summer. E, 3 × 3m/10 × 10ft

◆ *Where soil remains moist, and is prevented from drying out, flowering will be increased.*

Rosa glauca Striking grey-green foliage acts as a foil to small, pink flowers which are followed by colourful heps. 2 × 1.2m/6 × 4ft

Neillia thibetica Considering the ease of cultivation, it is surprising that this attractive shrub is not more widely grown. Flowers from April onwards. 2 × 2m/6 × 6ft

◆ *Neillia is suckering in habit. Unwanted growth may be cut out at ground level over the winter.*

***Lonicera periclymenum* 'Belgica'** Delicious, old-fashioned fragrance combines with good foliage on versatile honeysuckles which should be permitted to scramble at will. 7m/23ft

***Kolkwitzia amabilis* 'Pink Cloud'** A splendid addition to the back of the border, the graceful beauty bush is most aptly named. 3 × 3m/10 × 10ft

***Deutzia* × *elegantissima* 'Rosealind'** Once the flowers are over, remove dead wood and cut back old flowered stems by two thirds. 1 × 1.5m/3 × 5ft

***Lavatera* 'Barnsley'** This is a shrub for an open, sunny spot in free-draining soil. Given these conditions it will flower profusely for several months. 2 × 1m/6 × 3ft

◆ *In mid to late spring hard prune all stems to ground level. The hollyhock-type flowers are borne on the current season's growth.*

Phlomis fruticosa The Jerusalem sage carries whorls of brilliant yellow flowers from early summer onwards. Here it is teamed with *Campanula poscharskyana*. E, 1 × 1m/3 × 3ft

◆ *Following flowering, dead head. Restrict pruning to cutting back old or frost damaged stems in the spring to points of new growth.*

Lupinus arboreus Although these loose-growing shrubs are short-lived, they are easily propagated from seed and are quick to establish. Semi-E, 1.5 × 1.5m/ 5 × 5ft

***Brachyglottis (Senecio)* 'Sunshine'** This silvery-grey leafed shrub forms a compact dome. Daisy flowers of golden yellow mass the bush in June. ❍, E, 1 × 1.5m/ 3 × 5ft

Buddleja globosa Inflorescences on this early-flowering buddleja resemble orange balls and are unmistakably scented. 2.4 × 2m/ 8 × 6ft

***Rosa* 'Blanc Double de Coubert'** Papery blooms of purest white distinguish this fragrant rugosa rose. Flowers persist for the greater part of the summer. 1.5 × 1.2m/5 × 4ft

***Abutilon vitifolium* 'Album'** In early summer this wall-trained shrub is a mass of white, hollyhock-like flowers. Unsuitable for very cold, exposed gardens. ❍, 2.4m/8ft

Carpenteria californica A lovely shrub with bright, glossy foliage and beautifully scented white flowers with pronounced golden anthers in June and July. ❍, E, 1.5 × 1.5m/5 × 5ft

◆ *Cold winters will adversely affect carpenterias. However, in most cases they will regenerate with new shoots arising from the base of the plant in spring.*

***Clematis* 'Mrs. Cholmondeley'** Hard prune this clematis in the spring to promote lavender-blue flowers from early summer. Suitable for a pot or container. 3m/6ft

◆ *Other clematis for pot cultivation are 'Arctic Queen', 'Lady Northcliffe' and 'Mrs. P.B. Truax'. All will need some form of support.*

Buddleja alternifolia Graceful, arching stems carry scented lilac flowers in June. An exceptionally attractive shrub. Grow in a mixed border or as a specimen. ❍, 4 × 4m/13 × 13ft

GARDENS OPEN TO THE PUBLIC

Succumb to the temptation during these long days of summer to abandon working in the garden in favour of visiting one of many open to the public.

For the price of a small admission charge, often for charity, countless gardens, from the very tiny to the very large, open to visitors during the summer months. This is a wonderful opportunity to gain ideas, to discover new plants or simply to seek relaxation. Numerous publications listing gardens open to the public line the shelves of booksellers, so there is no difficulty in discovering what is open when.

Many, too, are combined with small nurseries allowing for the possibility of returning home with some new found treasure.

The formal design of this garden relies on total symmetry of hard and soft landscaping, both artfully controlled, to achieve its effect. Clever use is made of topiary, not only in the form of the golden balls but in the way in which the clipped spirals echo the pillars of the little summerhouse. Circles, suggested by pots, plants and the arrangement of granite sets, are deceptive in creating a feeling of space and openness in an area which might otherwise appear to close inwards.

As the season progresses, many gardens continue to have much of interest to offer the visitor. Here late summer perennials extend the season after the main June display.

Colours in this mixed border are thoughtfully combined to create a unified whole. The success of a scheme like this demands much in the way of good border management.

This long vista invites the visitor to explore, the archway in the distance acting as a magnet. Softly textured roses contrast with tightly clipped yew.

Illustrated here is just a small part of a much larger garden. However, it is often possible to adapt ideas and scale to fit a much smaller space.

THE KITCHEN GARDEN

Successional sowings of salad crops on a fortnightly basis will give a constant supply through the summer into autumn.

Lettuce may be sown in a bed in which they are to remain, transplanting only when there is overcrowding. Planting distances should be around 30cm/1ft.

Cabbage and celeriac may be planted out this month.

Cutting from established asparagus beds should be discontinued from the middle of the month.

SOW FOR NEXT YEAR

By June the ground should be sufficiently warm to allow for the sowing of herbaceous perennials and hardy biennials not sown in May.

Prepare a seed bed in a partially shaded area, working the soil to a fine tilth and then pressing down firmly. Leave to settle for a day or two before seeding.

Sow seed in drills, cover lightly and water using a fine rose. Within a few weeks seedlings should be large enough to thin out and transplant. Leave to develop fully in reserve beds which should be sunny, well dug and, if the soil is poor, enriched.

If required, hardy biennials like the *Dianthus barbatus*, sweet William, shown here may be sown where they are to flower.

WATERING

Water, that most precious of commodities, should never be wasted. There is no substitute for rainwater so any form of artificial watering should be limited and resorted to only where absolutely necessary.

Essential watering, carried out when the sun is down, should be applied directly, if at all possible, to the roots of each plant and not over foliage. Watering in the open – new plantings, newly turfed or seeded grass – must be done sufficiently thoroughly to wet the ground.

Plants in pots must, of course, receive regular watering and should never be allowed to dry out. In very hot periods, move them out of the sun.

SOFTWOOD CUTTINGS
Early summer is an ideal time in which to propagate shrubs, like this potentilla, by softwood cuttings just as the new shoots are beginning to ripen.

In taking cuttings strong, sturdy shoots should be removed from the plant and a clean cut made just below a joint. Where possible this cut should be two or three joints beneath the point from which foliage springs. Cuttings strike best when they have not too much foliage to bear – remove or shorten excess leaves.

Cuttings should be arranged around the edge of a pot containing an appropriate compost mixture. This may be made by mixing and sieving equal parts of leaf-mould, loam and sharp silver sand.

Water well and place in a cold frame in a shady situation. As cuttings strike, increase ventilation, harden off and pot up individually.

CHECK LIST

- Regularly dead head to prolong flowering period.
- Continue to cut and edge grass.
- Visit garden centres and nurseries to purchase new plants in flower (p.107).
- Check stakes of tall-growing perennials like delphiniums.
- Add colour to terrace or patio with Miniature or Patio roses in pots (p.117).
- Introduce additional climbers into the garden (pp.118 and 121).
- Visit gardens open to the public for inspiration (p.130).
- Sow herbaceous perennials for next year (p.132).
- Make fortnightly sowings of salad crops (p.132).
- Take softwood cuttings of shrubs (p.133).
- Check roses for pests and diseases. Spray if necessary.
- Prune late-spring flowering shrubs like *Kerria*.

TIDY BORDERS
Maintenance of borders, in the form of dead heading, cutting back, weeding where necessary, and checking stakes and ties, will ensure that the garden remains looking good as June moves into July.

JULY

MIDSUMMER, and the July garden is awash with colour. This is the month of red hot pokers, of flat headed yarrow, of long-flowering penstemons and diascias, of garden pinks and tall, border phlox. Summer bedding reaches a new intensity. Vibrant reds, golden yellows, indeed all the strong colours of the palette, combine to reflect the heat of the sun in this the hottest of months.

This is a month in which to relax, to enjoy not only the richness of the borders but also the delicious scents of summer. It is a time for sitting in the shade, for meals taken out of doors, for impromptu parties or simply absorbing the peace and stillness of the garden at the end of a busy day.

These parallel borders, seen in the early days of July, give an appearance of extravagant plenty whilst being very tightly controlled in terms of colour and plant mix. Large clumps of lime-green alchemilla and purple sage are used at intervals with confidence.

Although there is no intention that one side of the path should mirror the other, the use of the same and similar plants makes for a satisfying, unified whole.

***Epilobium angustifolium album/Lavatera* 'Barnsley'** A very effective and totally pleasing combination. White rosebay willow herb is teamed in this garden with the shrubby mallow to provide an interesting contrast of flower shape as well as colour. Both will be in bloom for many weeks. 1.2m × 60cm/4 × 2ft and 2 × 1m/6 × 3ft

◆ *Note how planting in this border matches the size and scale of the wall which backs it.*

Verbena bonariensis The low-growing shrub *Lavatera* 'Burgundy Wine' is encircled here by a haze of airy *Verbena bonariensis*. This tall, slender stemmed perennial will flower from July until October and is very effective when used as a 'see-through' plant at the front of the border. 1.2m × 15cm/4ft × 6in

***Penstemon* 'Apple Blossom'** Grow this pretty penstemon behind a pink-flowering lavender. Both enjoy good drainage and full sun. ❍, 45 × 45cm/1½ × 1½ft

***Campanula punctata* 'Rubriflora'** This is a very striking campanula to grow. Periodically check its spread by digging up unwanted runners. 30 × 30cm/1 × 1ft

◆ *Similar in form is* C. takesimana *but flowers are mottled, wine red over white, rather than single coloured.*

***Alstroemeria* hybrid** This rather shocking pink alstroemeria should, in theory, be a little too much. However, placed with care it makes a spectacular display. ❍, 60 × 30cm/2 × 1ft

◆ *'Ligtu hybrids' are to be found in colours to suit most tastes and to fit in with the majority of planting schemes.*

Osteospermum jucundum Whilst many osteospermums will succumb to frost, this one is relatively hardy and will, in time, form a spreading mat. ❍, 30 × 30cm/1 × 1ft

***Monarda* 'Cambridge Scarlet'** Spidery flowers are carried above strongly aromatic leaves. In recent years various new forms of bergamot have been introduced. ❍, 1 × 1m/3 × 3ft

***Anthemis tinctoria* 'Alba'** Repeated dead heading will encourage continuous flowering of this sun-loving perennial. An excellent form is *A. tinctoria* 'E.C. Buxton'. ❍, 75 × 75cm/2½ × 2½ft

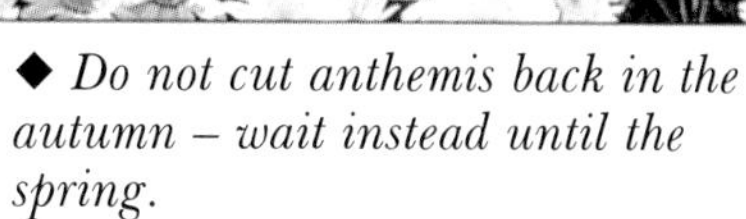

◆ *Do not cut anthemis back in the autumn – wait instead until the spring.*

Eryngium tripartitum Blue and spiky flowers are complemented by thistle-type foliage on this sea-holly. Pair it with an orange day lily. ❍, 45 × 25cm/1½ft × 10in

***Aster* × *frikartii* 'Mönch'** Starting to flower in July, this favourite Michaelmas daisy will add colour to the border for several months. ❍, 75 × 45cm/2½ × 1½ft

Convolvulus sabatius A charming addition to a gravel garden where its trailing stems should be allowed to spread outwards. Not completely hardy. ❍, 15 × 45cm/6in × 1½ft

Lysimachia punctata Lysimachia will thrive in most situations, often outgrowing its allotted space. However, it is not difficult to keep within bounds. 75 × 75cm/2½ × 2½ft

◆ *Look out for* L. ciliata *'Firecracker' whose foliage is a deep burgundy red. Avoid poor forms with paler leaves.*

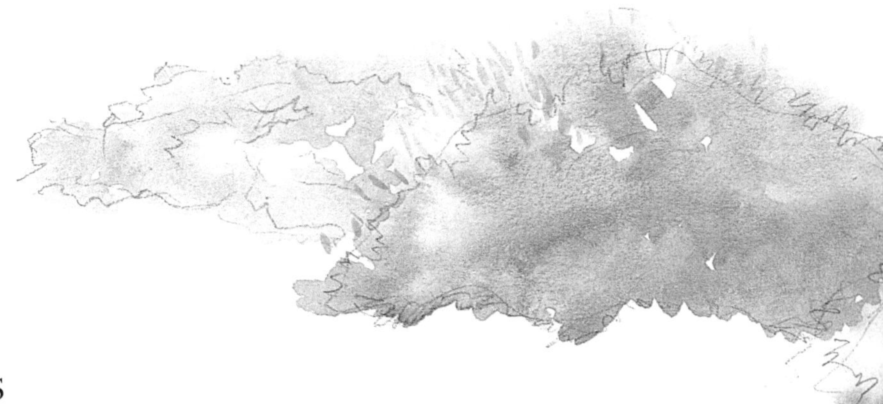

SCENTED PLANTS

Capture the perfumes of Arcadia by filling the July garden with scented plants. Fragrant pinks, heady lilies, tobacco plants, sweet-smelling stocks, lavender and southern-woods, each delights individually and together they contribute to a midsummer pot-pourri.

***Dianthus* 'Waithman Beauty'** A distinctive pink which is small enough to include in the rock garden or used to edge a much frequented path. ❍, E, 15 × 23cm/6 × 9in

Lilium candidum Who can resist the purity, and heavenly scent, of the Madonna lily? Ideal for pot cultivation where they can be given sharp drainage and water during the growing season. ❍, 1.2m/4ft

◆ *By growing lilies in containers, they may be moved into a prominent position for their flowering period.*

Pots of *Lilium regale* and tender *Acidanthera bicolor murielae* are placed here among lavenders and pinks to surround this seat with lovely summer fragrances. An additional pleasure will be had from the murmuring of many bees, inevitably drawn towards these aromatic plants.

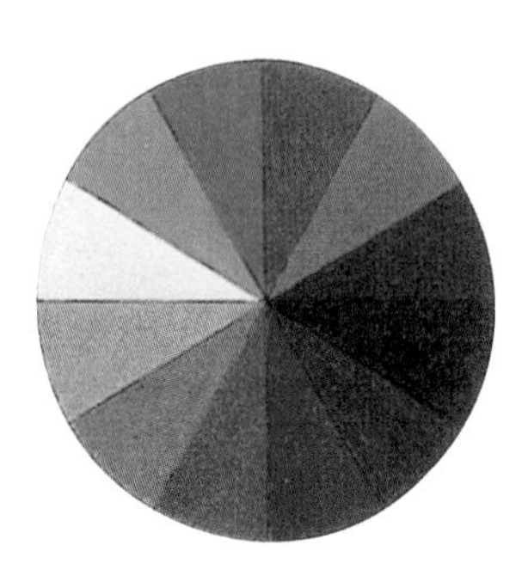

COLOUR WHEEL
Use the colour wheel to determine planting schemes. Adjacent colours, and those opposite each other, will go together and look well.

SUMMER SCHEMES – *White and Blue*

Sometimes change is called for. The traditional border, with its mixture of trees and shrubs, annuals and perennials of mixed colours continues to excite interest and remains understandably popular.

Borders in which the principal colours are restricted to one, two or possibly three, have a special appeal and underline a particular intent.

Experimentation with colour is endless. White gardens are firmly established in present day garden lore. Combining blue and white together, in varying degrees, is to modify a familiar theme and, by the thoughtful arrangement and juxtaposition of plants, is to break new ground.

***Phlox paniculata* 'White Admiral'** From late July into August and beyond this cool twinning of scented phlox and dark blue agapanthus, *Agapanthus* 'Loch Hope', will provide startling yet controlled border colour. 75 × 60cm/2½ × 2ft

◆ *Agapanthus, or African lilies, will benefit from a regular application of liquid manure during the growing season.*

Campanula alliariifolia A rather dreamy campanula with long flower bells held to one side of the tall stem. This perennial prefers moist soil. ◐, 75 × 45cm/2½ × 1½ft

Eryngium bourgatii Somewhat resembling a very superior form of thistle, this sea-holly provides a welcome contrast of texture and form. ❍, 60 × 30cm/2 × 1ft

Campanula persicifolia White, blue and double forms of this campanula account for its good reputation. A self-seeder, it never becomes a nuisance. ❍, 1m × 30cm/3 × 1ft

Campanula poscharskyana An indispensable rockery campanula which will spread about into cracks and crevices without becoming invasive. Dead heading is very simple. Pull the flower stems which come away easily to leave a mat of fresh green foliage. It will continue flowering until the frosts arrive. 25 × 60cm/ 10in × 2ft

***Solanum jasminoides* 'Album'** Introduce this amazingly lovely climber as a backdrop to any border where white is the dominant colour. Inclined to be tender. ❍, Semi-E, 6m/20ft

Salvia patens The bright blue flowers are almost without equal in the summer months. Apply a thick mulch over the crown for winter protection. ❍, 60 × 45cm/2 × 1½ft

***Lathyrus latifolius* 'White Pearl'** Sweet peas are an essential part of summer. This perennial climber could be wall trained or allowed to romp through the border. ❍, 2m/6ft

***Veronica austriaca* 'Shirley Blue'** Plant either in groups or arrange as a ribbon to thread through a white border. 'Shirley Blue' has a tendency to flop a little so is excellent where informality is the order. ❍, 20 × 30cm/8in × 1ft

◆ *After flowering, crop close to the ground. New foliage, and possibly more flowers, will quickly form.*

Campanula latiloba alba Cool white bell flowers create a moody, enticing atmosphere when placed in a lightly shaded spot. Use this campanula as a mainstay of a white border. *C. latiloba* is studded with lavender-blue flowers. 1.2m × 30cm/4 × 1ft

◆ *Basal rosettes are evergreen. To tidy the plant, just remove spent flower stalks.*

SUMMER SCHEMES – *Red and Yellow*

Placing red and yellow together takes some daring and would certainly not be to everyone's taste. Recent years have seen much emphasis in gardens on pale pastel schemes, so a return to something more vibrant is both innovative and challenging. Fiery, hot borders are increasingly fashionable and when flaming annuals are added to perennials, then the garden is truly ablaze.

Abutilon megapotamicum A spectacular shrub to grow against a warm wall in full sun. Conspicuous, and rather strange, red and yellow flowers which appear from early June could not be bettered for a hot scheme. Numerous garden hybrids are obtainable. ❍, E, 2.4m/8ft

◆ *Abutilon should be pruned in spring by the removal of dead or frosted wood. All forms may be propagated from cuttings.*

Potentilla fruticosa A cheery little shrub which is never without a mass of flower during the summer months. 1.2 × 1.2m/ 4 × 4ft

Callistemon rigidus Unusual 'bottle brushes' are carried above lemon-scented foliage. This is a shrub for a well drained, acidic soil in full sun. ❍, E, 3m/10ft

Hypericum calycinum The buttery yellow flowers of Rose of Sharon are most appealing and the plant will grow almost anywhere but can be invasive. E, 30cm/1ft

Tropaeolum speciosum Plant this splendid climber with its brilliant scarlet flowers to grow against a dark background. Here it climbs into a yew hedge. By the time the hedge needs cutting, the flowers will be over. 2m/6ft

◆ *Tropaeolum will disappear completely during the winter. It may be necessary to mark its position with a cane.*

Tropaeolum majus Garden nasturtiums are fast-growing annuals providing a mass of flowers in yellows, oranges and crimsons. Sow seed in spring, ❍, 30 × 30cm/1 × 1ft

***Canna* 'Fireside'** Intensely dramatic cannas are suggestive of sunsets in the tropics. They should be afforded protection from frost. ❍, 75 × 30cm/2½ × 1ft

***Penstemon* 'Chester Scarlet'** This particular penstemon has proved itself to be reliably hardy. Plant in a mass for impact. ❍, 60 × 45cm/2 × 1½ft

Lilium pardalinum A planting of leopard lilies with their nodding turkscap flowers will revel in the summer sun. ❍, 2m × 30cm/ 6 × 1ft

◆ *This is one of the most beautiful summer plants and may grow to 3m/10ft.*

A hot border such as this one will be alight from early summer right through until autumn. The last rose, 'Just Joey', contrasts with the flat heads of achillea whilst the red and orange crocosmias will remain in flower for weeks on end. In the foreground the round blooms of the dahlia are partnered with the tassels of amaranthus, love-lies-bleeding.

SUMMER SCHEMES – *Lemon and Purple*

Purple, in isolation, may appear somewhat oppressive, dowdy even, so that in a small area the overall effect could be one of dullness and general gloom. Add yellow, from the palest of tints to deep lemon, and the border is electrified, immediately brought to life. Where a softer, less positive outcome is intended, use dusky lilacs and lavenders. For something bolder and stronger, introduce magenta.

Few would quarrel with this very successful companion planting. Washed out yellow hollyhocks, *Alcea rugosa*, intermingle with generous groupings of *Penstemon* 'Alice Hindley', whilst the deeper shades of *Clematis* 'Perle d'Azur' reinforce this deliberately restricted colour scheme. Bracts of *Euphorbia amygdaloides* var. *robbiae* are in complete harmony.

A border like this one could be easily underplanted with spring bulbs, narcissus, crocus and tulips, using similar tones.

***Oenothera* 'Fireworks'** A fairly compact perennial evening primrose of a bright yellow. Flowers throughout the midsummer. ❍, 45 × 30cm/ 1½ × 1ft

◆ *As an alternative, try the self-seeding biennial,* O. biennis.

Clematis × durandii Deep indigo flowers will appear throughout July and August on this clematis which is best trained through a small shrub. 2.4m/8ft

Helichrysum italicum The curry plant, technically a herb, tones beautifully here with lavender-blue catmint and a magenta geranium. ❍, 60 × 60cm/2 × 2ft

***Clematis* 'Victoria'** Rosy-purple *Clematis* 'Victoria' enjoys the same situation as the day lily, *Hemerocallis* 'Whichford'. The climber, of course, needs support. 3.5m/12ft

***Kniphofia* 'Little Maid'** An excellent plant for introducing variation in form. These creamy-yellow pokers are well suited to the small garden. 60 × 45cm/ 2 × 1½ft

◆ *Associate these pokers with one of the midsummer asters such as the lilac* Aster thompsonii *'Nanus'.*

This sunny spot has been exploited to the full. Scrambling through and beyond the climber *Rosa* 'Golden Showers' are the rich purple flowers of the vigorous *Solanum crispum* 'Glasnevin', whose yellow central points pick up exactly the tones of the rose. Not only is the rose scented, but so too are the madonna lilies which surround it. Little wonder that this is seen as a place to site a garden seat.

Lonicera tragophylla In total contrast to the solanum, this warmly coloured honeysuckle will happily climb and flower in total shade. Unfortunately the delightfully formed flowers are without scent. That apart, this climber is well worth seeking out. ●, 6m/20ft

SUMMER BEDDING

By July summer bedding, in place now for several weeks, should be filling out to provide an ongoing display. Schemes planned over several months mature by midsummer and should delight with continuous colour and interest right through until the first frosts of autumn.

During prolonged dry spells it may become necessary to water shallow-rooted bedding plants. The application of a liquid fertilizer will extend the flowering period, as will regular dead heading.

A series of raised beds has been used here as home to a range of bedding plants. These include impatiens, nicotiana and ageratum, all arranged in linear composition. Careful consideration of height needs to be given to an arrangement of this kind. Taller plants must not block those which are lower growing.

Nicotiana enjoy a sunny situation where they will flower all summer long. During the evening they are particularly noticeable for their fragrance. ○, 30 × 15cm/ 1ft × 6in

Chrysanthemum parthenium Most suitable for edging a path or, with its aromatic leaves, to include in the kitchen or herb garden. ❍, 23 × 15cm/9 × 6in

Antirrhinum Snapdragons continue to remain favourite cottage garden plants. Reasonably hardy, they may well survive a mild winter. ❍, 30 × 15cm/1ft × 6in

Impatiens For spectacular colour and free flowering few other bedding plants are able to rival impatiens, or busy lizzie. They will tolerate some shade. 30 × 15cm/1ft × 6in

A carefully co-ordinated arrangement of summer bedding where colours are restricted yet plantings are generous. *Chrysanthemum parthenium* is used to edge the bed with *Salvia splendens* and impatiens weaving a ribbon of colour around evergreen conifer and hebe.

***Argyranthemum* 'Vancouver'** Pretty marguerites lend themselves to informal situations, for filling gaps left by early-flowering perennials. ❍, 1 × 1m/3 × 3ft

Centaurea cyanus Grow cornflowers where plants are allowed to self-seed and the emphasis is on the natural rather than the formal. ❍, 45 × 15cm/1½ft × 6in

Heliotrope Strongly scented flowers, smelling of cooked cherries, over deeply veined, dark green leaves. Good for either formal or informal schemes. ❍, 45 × 15cm/1½ft × 6in

A most successful use of summer bedding. Contrast of colour, variation of height, carefully arranged drifts of plants and an apparent simplicity are the principal ingredients of this very attractive border.

In the main plants are restricted to triphylla fuchsias and *Argyranthemum* 'Jamaica Primrose'. Neither will, of course, withstand frost.

The tall-growing *Nicotiana* 'Sensation' and the large double flowers of zinnia in an informal bedding scheme.

***Rosa filipes* 'Kiftsgate'** Where space is unlimited this wonderful white rose, with individual shoots of 6m/20ft or more, will create an amazing, breath-taking cascade of flower in midsummer. Not, it should be stressed, for anywhere other than a huge area.

◆ *Much less vigorous is* Rosa *'Bobbie James' (10 × 7m/33 × 23ft) which will happily grow through an old apple tree.*

SHRUBS AND TREES

Scent remains a dominant force among the trees and shrubs of July. From wonderfully fragrant honeysuckles, among them the common *Lonicera periclymenum*, to aromatic lavenders and the pineapple-scented *Cytisus battandieri*, there is something for every garden however large or small. And where there is no scent, there is certainly no absence of flower.

***Lonicera periclymenum* 'Serotina'** An exceedingly attractive honeysuckle with an enticing perfume which will succeed in both sun or part shade in any ordinary garden soil. As an alternative, choose *L.* × *americana* which is equally scented. 7m/23ft

◆ *In the wild honeysuckles are often to be found in hedgerows. An informal hedge could play host to one in the garden.*

Indigofera heterantha Place this compact shrub in a hot, dry spot to be rewarded with flower from midsummer into autumn. ❍, 2 × 2m/6 × 6ft

Hebe The summer-flowering hebes will delight with their soft colours and evergreen foliage. In spring, remove any frost-damaged growth. E, 45cm × 1m/ 1½ × 3ft

***Lavandula angustifolia* 'Hidcote'** One of the best known lavenders with deeply coloured flower spikes. Dead head after flowering and cut back in spring. ❍, E, 60 × 45cm/2 × 1½ft

Lavatera maritima bicolor The unusual flower colour of this tree mallow is very appealing. Flowers appear on the current season's growth so all stems should be hard pruned to the ground in spring. 2 × 1m/6 × 3ft

◆ *This shrub could very easily be planted close to a wall and trained as if a climber.*

Cytisus battandieri The beautifully scented flowers of this shrub make it very desirable, but also the silky, silvery leaves. Place in a warm situation. Semi-E, 5 × 5m/16 × 16ft

Sorbaria tomentosa var. ***angustifolia*** Elegant white plumes over finely cut foliage on this moisture-loving shrub. In autumn leaves turn a pleasant yellow. 3 × 3m/10 × 10ft

***Escallonia* 'Iveyi'** Less widely grown than the pink escallonias, the white flowered 'Iveyi' is best afforded a little shelter from winter winds. E, 4 × 3m/13 × 10ft

Genista aetnensis The Mount Etna broom is a mass of sunny flowers at this time and would be splendid at the back of a border. 4 × 4m/13 × 13ft

◆ *Little attention need be given to this broom beyond a light clipping after flowering.*

CONTAINERS

Pots and containers planted up in May are now satisfying all their past promise. Gathered together in groups, for ease of watering, or placed strategically around the garden, they add instant colour or serve as focal points.

Lilies in particular are made for pot cultivation. By growing them in containers they may be given the good drainage they demand, water during the growing season and, not least, the prominence which is their due when in flower.

An old lead cistern has been utilized here as a home for pelargoniums and a purple leafed cotinus. The pelargoniums will be changed annually but the shrub may remain.

One of the most important aspects of pot cultivation is to provide adequate drainage. Ensure a good supply of crocks in any container.

***Begonia semperflorens* 'Kalinka Rose'** These tuberous begonias fill this attractively swagged clay pot which may be sited in sun or shade. 60cm × 1m/2 × 3ft

White petunias and blue lobelia enhance rather than detract from the simple dignity of this stone trough.

Schizanthus A very pretty pot arrangement using a popular annual. To encourage a bushy plant, pinch out the growing tips early on.

Care has been taken in this welcoming sitting-out area to keep plants in pots of similar tones. This reinforces a feeling of restfulness which is appropriate to the surroundings.

The hornbeam hedge behind the seat not only traps the sun but also the scent of the lilies.

Cheery pansies are teamed up in this trough with lobelia to give a long lasting summer display.

◆ *Once again, colours have been deliberately selected to harmonize with one another.*

This beautifully weathered stone urn has been filled with a white argyranthemum.

Agave americana The succulent century plant with its sharp, sword-like leaves is not, sadly, hardy. Housed over winter in a frost-free environment, it takes pride of place for the season in a small, enclosed court. 1 × 1m/3 × 3ft

◆ *Surrounding the agave in its terracotta pot, and providing a splash of colour, is* Verbena *'Homestead Purple'.*

***Fuchsia* 'Tennessee Waltz'** With its upright, arching habit this makes a magnificent pot specimen. Double flowers are pink and lavender-rose. ◐, 1m × 75cm/3 × 2½ft

Brugmansia Angel's Trumpet, if well grown, make an impressive plant. It may, if required, be cultivated as a standard. 1.2 × 1m/4 × 3ft

***Fuchsia* 'Rufus the Red'** The bright red flowers are single and are produced in profusion during the flowering season. ◐, 1.5m × 75cm/5 × 2½ft

***Lilium* 'Stargazer'** Of all the oriental hybrid lilies, the popularity of 'Stargazer' is never in question. Upright crimson-red flowers, a spicy fragrance and long-lasting blooms are the qualities which have proved its worth. 1.2–2m/4–6ft

◆ *Each autumn, after the flowers have died down, top dress lilies with garden compost or leaf mould.*

***Lilium* 'Mont Blanc'** A pure white lily. Plant in clumps of three, five, seven or more for a better display. 75cm–1m/2½–3ft

Lilium regale For many, this particular lily, with its sweet scent and elegant flowers flushed yellow, is without rival. 1.2–2m/4–6ft

***Lilium* 'Pink Perfection'** Large trumpet flowers of deep pink. As with all lilies, plant deeply in pots or the open ground and give good drainage. 1.5m/5ft

THE PONDSIDE

At the pond's edge, relishing the damp, moisture loving astilbes, rodgersias and summer flowering primulas jostle for attention. More than at any other time of the year, this part of the garden now enjoys a feeling of plenty, made possible by generous plantings of ferns, grasses, hostas, rushes, as well as flowering meadowsweet (*Filipendula*), day lilies (*Hemerocallis*) and late irises.

Bold drifts of astilbes and irises around this pond ensure continuous colour, as well as good foliage effect. *Iris pseudacorus* (Yellow flag) has finished flowering but the odd *I. sibirica* keeps going. The main display is of white *Astilbe* 'Deutschland' with pink *A.* 'Erica' behind.

◆ *Note how the pond's surface is planted with water lilies to reduce the problem of algae.*

Effective planting demonstrating a variety of form and texture. The foliage of tall, strappy irises contrasts with that of the geraniums in the foreground and the pink flowered astilbes behind. Silver leafed artemisia acts as a foil to the pinky-red of *Berberis* 'Rose Glow' on the left, whilst the bronze form of the sedge *Carex comans* softens the edge of the path.

Ferns, hostas and summer primula, *Primula florindae*, are the mainstays of this scheme for the margins of a pond. Golden leaves of *Carex elata* 'Aurea' artfully pick up the same colour tones of the primula. In a poolside garden many subjects provide a harmonious setting for the succession of flowering plants through the shapes and healthy greens of their leaves.

Deep red plumes of *Astilbe* 'Montgomery' make a bold, dramatic statement in this planting scheme around a narrow stream. Strong patterns like this can only be achieved by grouping several plants of the same form rather than planting them singly. In winter both foliage and flowers will have died down to reveal the water.

Ligularia przewalskii At home in any garden soil which is moisture retentive. This is a spreading perennial so allow ample space. 1.2 × 1m/4 × 3ft

◆ *This ligularia will start in flower in July and continue well into autumn.*

***Hemerocallis* 'Bonanza'** All the day lilies are tolerant of most soils and situations with the exception of dry shade. 1m × 75cm/3 × 2½ft

***Zantedeschia aethiopica* 'Crowborough'** These striking arum-type flowers need to be grown in very damp conditions. Cover crowns in winter for protection. 60 × 60cm/2 × 2ft

Primula florindae Citrus-yellow bell flowers of this moisture-loving primula carry a distinct scent and are in flower for many weeks. ◐, 75 × 75cm/2½ × 2½ft

***Rodgersia pinnata* 'Superba'** Thick, deeply etched leaves are as remarkable as the soft pink flowers. This plant is excellent where an accent on foliage is required. 1 × 1m/3 × 3ft

***Polygonum* (syn. *Persicaria*) *affine* 'Superbum'** Use this as a carpet around trees and shrubs. Pink-white poker flowers mature crimson. 20 × 30cm/8in × 1ft

Primula vialii These pointed lavender-pink flowers are bright scarlet in bud. An unusual primula for damp soil. 30 × 30cm/1 × 1ft

***Filipendula rubra* 'Venusta'** Sometimes mistaken for an astilbe. Meadowsweet is an excellent plant for the water's edge and will colonize rapidly. 1.5m × 75cm/5 × 2½ft

◆ Filipendula purpurea alba *is an attractive white form for any damp situation.*

DRYING HERBS AND FLOWERS
Gather herbs and flowers for drying during a warm period when they are free from moisture. Cut stems cleanly, arrange in thin bunches and hang upside down in an airy place at an even temperature to dry. Suitable plants include bergamots, chives, flax, lavender, oregano and teasels. Later these bunches may be arranged to form interesting and attractive displays indoors over the winter months.

THE KITCHEN GARDEN
Onions and shallots should soon be ready to harvest. Before doing this, bend the tops over to prevent seeding and to allow for maximum sunlight on the onions themselves.

After lifting, spread out under cover to dry completely before putting into store. Onions may either be stored in boxes or in the more traditional way by roping together. Which ever way, they should keep well for several months.

Other jobs include cleaning and tidying strawberry beds and summer pruning of fruit trees. Where fruit appears to be overcrowded, thin accordingly.

Continue successional sowings of crops like beetroot, summer lettuce, radish, salad onion, spinach. These should mature before the first frosts but are likely to be the last crops that do so.

PROPAGATION BY LAYERING
July is the usual month for propagating by this easy, sure method although other times of year will do equally well.

Make an upward cut just below a joint on a lower stem or shoot of a plant to be propagated. This incision should open the stem to about the centre when it should be placed in contact with the earth. Peg it down and pile soil over, firming well. The outer end of the shoot, beyond the cut, should be trained upwards.

When the layer has rooted it should be cut away from the parent plant and potted up or planted out.

LIFT SPRING BULBS
Spring bulbs, such as daffodils and tulips, will have now died down. These may be lifted, if required, cleaned, dried off and stored in a cool, dry place in readiness for replanting in the autumn.

CHECK LIST

- Arrange scented plants in pots on patio or terrace (p.138).
- Consider colour theme borders (pp.140–151).
- Continue programme of dead heading.
- Feed and water summer bedding (p.152).
- Attend regularly to container-grown plants (p.160).
- Dry herbs and flowers for decorative use (p.168).
- Harvest onions and shallots (p.168).
- Clean up strawberry beds (p.168).
- Summer prune fruit trees (p.168).
- Continue successional sowings of vegetables (p.168).
- Propagate by layering (p.169).
- Lift spring bulbs (p.169).

ATTEND TO ROSES
Go through rose beds and borders towards the end of the month. Dead head and tidy rose bushes and then apply a general fertilizer. This should keep them in good condition into autumn and, in some instances, encourage a repeat flowering.

AUGUST

HIGH SUMMER and holidays. August is a time of transition, a link between the secure days of summer and the onset of autumn. But borders need not be dull. Already late flowering perennials are making a show and colourful annuals have many weeks yet to run.

Temperatures often remain high and inevitably some plants will show signs of being under stress. Water only if absolutely essential, and then ensure that water is sufficient to reach and saturate roots. Lawns may well be parched and brown. This should not cause concern for the first of the autumn rains will quickly restore them to their original colour and vitality.

Weeds should no longer present much of a problem, particularly if the tiresome but necessary chore of weeding has been carried out regularly during preceding months. Make time to sit and enjoy the garden while summer lasts.

As this cottage garden demonstrates with a blaze of colour, there is much still to play for. An enthusiastic mix of annuals and perennials results in a bright display which will remain looking good right into autumn. Fuchsias, petunias, orange crocosmias, tagetes and dahlias are but a few of the many plants which contribute to this scene.

A garden such as this is by no means maintenance free. Regular dead heading, feeding and watering of containers must all be carried out.

***Helianthus* 'Monarch'** Sunflowers are fun to grow and look very splendid soaring upwards at the back of a border. ❍, 2.1 × 1m/ 7 × 3ft

◆ *Obviously perennials growing to this height require firm staking. See that it is in place at the start of the growing season.*

***Dendranthema* 'Nathalie'** One of very many cultivars of what were formerly known as chrysanthemums. These will continue well into autumn. 90cm/3ft

***Helenium* 'Moerheim Beauty'** The long-lasting mahogany coloured flowers of this late summer perennial anticipate the tints of autumn. ❍, 1m × 60cm/ 3 × 2ft

***Crocosmia* 'Mount Usher'** All crocosmias, and there are many desirable named forms, come into their own at this time. They prefer a sunny site. ❍, 60 × 30cm/2 × 1ft

Alcea rosea Hollyhocks have always had a place in the cottage garden. Available in a wide range of colours, including near black. 2m × 60cm/6 × 2ft

◆ *Grow hollyhocks against the wall of a house or a fence for a traditional appearance.*

***Lobelia cardinalis* 'Queen Victoria'** An exceedingly striking perennial. These intense red flowers are in bloom for several weeks. ❍, 90 × 30cm/3 × 1ft

◆ *In the late autumn cover the crowns with a thick mulch of garden compost to give added protection against frost.*

***Fuchsia magellanica* 'Gracilis Variegata'** Variegated leaves tone with the slender flowers of this hardy fuchsia. Avoid cutting back until the spring. 75 × 75cm/ 2½ × 2½ft

***Liatris spicata* 'Kobold'** A very pretty perennial for the later part of the summer. Slightly formal flower heads are held on stiff stems. 60 × 45cm/2 × 1½ft

All too often hardy fuchsias are overlooked for inclusion in the late summer border. In fact there is no reason why they should not be a major contributor, for their availability in colours from the softest to the richest makes them suitable for virtually any scheme. Added to that they flower for weeks on end.

In this border the red and purple flowers of *Fuchsia* 'Mrs. Popple' complement the deep blue of *Aconitum carmichaelii* and tone with the sombre leaves of the purple sage.

This particular bedding scheme, which makes use of brightly coloured African marigolds to surround a young monkey puzzle tree, *Araucaria*, will remain as dazzling as this until the first of the frosts.

◆ *Similar long-term colour could equally be provided with dahlias (see page 184) which are only now beginning to flower in earnest.*

Calendula Once used as a kitchen herb, marigold is now grown as an easy summer bedding plant. Thrives on poor soil. ○, 45cm/1½ft

Tagetes erecta Double ball-shaped blooms typify African marigolds in colours which range from pale lemon to deepest orange. Best in full sun. ○, 75cm/2½ft

Petunia Not only are showy petunias suitable for bedding, they are also useful to include in window boxes, pots and hanging baskets. ○, 15–45cm/6in–1½ft

Acanthus spinosissimus Both the purple hooded bracts and the foliage carry spines on this form of bear's breeches. ❍, 1.2m × 75cm/4 × 2½ft

***Clematis heracleifolia* 'Wyevale'** Treat this herbaceous clematis as any other perennial by cutting hard back in the autumn. 1 × 1m/3 × 3ft

***Sedum* 'Ruby Glow'** Sedums provide continuous colour over several weeks at this time. This will make a crimson carpet for an open, sunny spot. ❍, 30 × 30cm/1 × 1ft

***Echinops* 'Taplow Blue'** An impressive stand of the globe thistle planted as a drift through the back of this predominantly blue border. Globular flower heads may be as large as 7½cm/3in across. 1.5m × 60cm/5 × 2ft

◆ *Although this is the start of August,* Delphinium × bella-donna *'Peace' is still flowering well.*

Casual elegance is achieved in this planting scheme where much care has been taken to co-ordinate colour and to introduce variety of texture and form.

Providing necessary height at the back of the border is *Tamarix ramosissima*, its feathery rose-pink flowers of late summer conveying a feeling of softness. Central to the arrangement is a bold clump of *Phormium tenax* with its distinctive, sword-like leaves, the whole surrounded by a rugosa rose. Far right, *Fuchsia* 'Riccartonii' flowers alongside *Escallonia rubra* 'Crimson Spire'. All of the plants surrounding this inviting seat are suitable for growing at the seaside. Many, once established, will require little maintenance beyond some routine pruning.

For those living inland, thoughts in August invariably turn to those of the seaside. Gentle blue seas, warm golden sands and coastal walks all form part of this picture. But for those who garden on the coast life is not necessarily the idyll dreamed of by so many. True, a milder climate does allow the gardener to experiment with growing many plants which might well succumb to cold in less favourable areas. Both frost and snow are less of a likely hazard and there is not so much need to be conscious of providing tender plants with winter protection.

On the other hand, strong salt-laden winds whipping off the sea are capable of causing considerable damage to all but the most stalwart of plants. For this reason the planting of a shelter belt becomes of strategic importance. Initially fast growing conifers may be used as protection for trees which take more time to mature. Later the conifers can be removed.

SHRUBS AND TREES

Late flowering trees and shrubs, of which there is a plentiful supply, contribute a wide range of seasonal colour to the August garden. Lovely lace-cap hydrangeas, summer ceanothus and exciting hibiscus are all shrubs worthy of a place in the border.

Koelreuteria paniculata (*left*)
Pride of India or Golden rain tree are two of the names given to this handsome, medium-sized tree which bears panicles of small, yellow flowers during August. In autumn, as the leaves turn, the flowers are followed by bladder-like fruits. 13 × 8m/43 × 26ft

Eucryphia* × *nymansensis
Spectacular in flower. This highly ornamental tree should be placed in a situation where it is protected from cold winds. E, 14 × 4m/46 × 13ft

Hydrangea aspera (syn. ***villosa***) One of the loveliest of all the lace-cap hydrangeas with blooms of faded lilac-blue. Plant in a semi-shaded spot in acidic or neutral soil. Hydrangeas, both mop-head and lace-cap, need moisture at the roots. 2.4 × 2m/8 × 6ft

◆ Hydrangea villosa *looks stunning when underplanted with* Hosta lancifolia. *They share a similar coloured flower.*

***Hydrangea macrophylla* 'Veitchii'** Suitable for most garden soils as lime-tolerant. Blue flowers with outer florets of white fading to pink. 2 × 2.7m/6 × 9ft

***Hydrangea macrophylla* 'Hamburg'** Where conditions are alkaline the flowers are rose-pink. On more acidic soils the colour will deepen to purple-rose. 2 × 2.4m/6 × 8ft

***Hydrangea macrophylla* 'Ayesha'** Leaves are glossy green and the flowers are lilac-pink. Hydrangeas make excellent shrubs for containers provided they are kept well watered. 1 × 1.5m/3 × 5ft

***Perovskia atriplicifolia* 'Blue Spire'** A graceful shrub with lavender-blue flowers and grey foliage. The Russian sage should be hard pruned to ground level in spring. 1.5 × 1m/5 × 3ft

◆ *Planted in a group, this shrub would form a lovely hazy mist of blue.*

Yucca gloriosa One of the most architectural of plants and absolutely splendid in flower. Grow in pots or containers or to provide a statement of form in the border. The tips of the leaves are very sharp, hence the name Spanish dagger. E, trunk to 2m/6ft – flower to 2.4m/8ft

Itea ilicifolia Remarkable on account of the long, drooping flower racemes which appear from midsummer. Grow against a warm wall. E, 3 × 3m/10 × 10ft

Caryopteris* × *clandonensis A similar effect to perovskia and requiring the same pruning treatment. Named forms include 'Arthur Simmonds' and 'Heavenly Blue'. ❍, 80 × 80cm/ $2^1/_2 \times 2^1/_2$ft

◆ *A recent introduction is* C. *'Worcester Gold' with golden foliage.*

***Aralia elata* 'Variegata'** A mature example of the Japanese angelica tree is, understandably, highly prized. White flowers, appearing in late summer, are combined with silver-white leaves. Although hardy, it is advisable to place where the leaves will not be caught by late frost. 3.5 × 3m/ 12 × 10ft

***Hibiscus syriacus* 'Blue Bird'** These single violet-blue flowers cover this shrub during August and September. 'Diana' is a single, pure white form whilst 'Lady Stanley' possesses nearly double white flowers flushed maroon. No regular pruning is required. Remove dead or damaged shoots in spring. ❍, 2 × 2m/6 × 6ft

***Ceanothus* × *delileanus* 'Gloire de Versailles'** From July onwards a mature bush is heaped with light powder blue panicles of flowers. 2 × 2m/6 × 6ft

◆ *Try too the cultivar 'Perle Rose' which flowers at the same time but in rosy-pink.*

***Magnolia grandiflora* 'Exmouth'** A summer-flowering magnolia which will, in time, grow to be a large tree. E, 10 × 10m/33 × 33ft

Buddleja davidii Not surprisingly this type of buddleja is referred to as the butterfly bush for butterflies flock around it during summer. Hard pruned in spring, it grows rapidly to flower on the current season's growth. 4 × 4 m/13 × 13ft

◆ *Recommended are dark violet* B. d. *'Black Knight', red-purple 'Royal Red' and lilac-pink 'Pink Pearl'.*

***Clematis viticella* 'Purpurea Plena Elegans'** Grow this charming double clematis through a small shrub, such as *Hebe rakaiensis*, or team it with the plum coloured fruits of *Callicarpa bodinieri giraldii*. 3.5m/12ft

***Clematis texensis* 'Etoile Rose'** For some reason this lovely clematis is difficult to acquire. Best when allowed to scramble into a shrub or small tree. 2m/6ft

***Clematis viticella* 'Etoile Violette'** Imagine this deep purple flower in association with a golden leafed shrub. It should start to flower in July and continue well into September. 4m/3ft

◆ *The viticella group of clematis, all late-flowering, should be hard pruned in spring (see page 26).*

Schizophragma integrifolium Use this ornamental climber to cover an old tree stump or to grow against a wall. Creamy white flowers are produced in July and August. ❍, 6m/20ft

◆ *For most flowers,* Schizophragma *should be planted in full sun.*

Polygonum baldschuanicum Often used to cover an unsightly building, the Russian vine will smother any structure very rapidly. ❍, 12m/39ft

THE KITCHEN GARDEN
From the middle of the month begin successional sowings of spring cabbages for winter harvest. Keep seed beds moist and occasionally give a dusting of lime. After six weeks, or thereabouts, plants should be ready for transplanting to previously prepared ground. Water regularly.

Winter lettuce may be sown from August until October although later sowings should be made under glass. Give some protection to outdoor crops in hard weather.

SEMI-RIPE CUTTINGS
New shoots on plants are ideal to take as cutting material during August and September.

Choose sturdy, half mature side shoots, no longer than is necessary, and make a straight cut immediately below a joint. Remove any leaves from the lower half.

Dip the bottom of the cutting into hormone rooting powder and insert around the side of a pot filled with a suitable cutting compost. Firm in place. Water carefully and place in a cold frame and leave over winter.

By spring plants should have rooted and be ready to transplant into open ground where they may be brought on in a shady area.

GROWING DAHLIAS
Dahlias, one of the principal supporters of the late summer garden, are easily grown in open ground. In very warm districts they may be left to overwinter in position, a mounded heap of compost over the tubers acting as sufficient protection. More often, though, tubers are lifted as soon as frosts brown the foliage.

When this happens, cut off all but about 15cm/6in of stem and hang, stem down, to dry completely for a few days. Plunge into a box of ash or sand and store free from damp, frost and heat.

Dahlias are best propagated from overwintered tubers in March or April (see page 61).

PRUNE SUMMER-FLOWERING SHRUBS

Shrubs, like deutzia, philadelphus and weigela, indeed those which have flowered during the months of June, July and the beginning of August may be pruned now or as soon as they have finished flowering.

Shorten any exceptionally long shoots above a bud to give a tidy appearance to the shrub, then remove about one third of the oldest stems.

The main purpose of this pruning is one of renewal, to encourage a constant supply of new shoots and to prevent the shrub from becoming crowded with old and dead wood.

Now should also be the time to prune Rambler roses – that is, when they have finished flowering. Prune all stems that have flowered to ground level. Train and tie in new shoots as they develop.

Feed and mulch following pruning.

PLACE BULB ORDERS

As spring bulbs begin to appear in garden centres and nurseries, and exciting catalogues fall through the letterbox, now is the time to place orders.

Consult notes made earlier on (see page 71) and order immediately to avoid disappointment.

CHECK LIST

- Water any plants showing signs of stress (p.170).
- Include hardy fuchsias in late summer borders (p.173).
- Consider hydrangeas for pot cultivation (p.179).
- Cultivate dahlias for colour into autumn (p.184).
- Make sowings of winter cabbage and lettuce (p.184).
- Take semi-ripe cuttings (p.184).
- Prune summer-flowering shrubs, including Rambler roses (p.185).
- Order spring bulbs (p.185).

CLIP HEDGES

This is the month to trim hedges and to shape topiary. Where possible clip hedges with gently sloping sides to encourage a well furnished look to the ground. Aim to complete this job before bad weather sets in. Always use a line to ensure a crisp, straight finish.

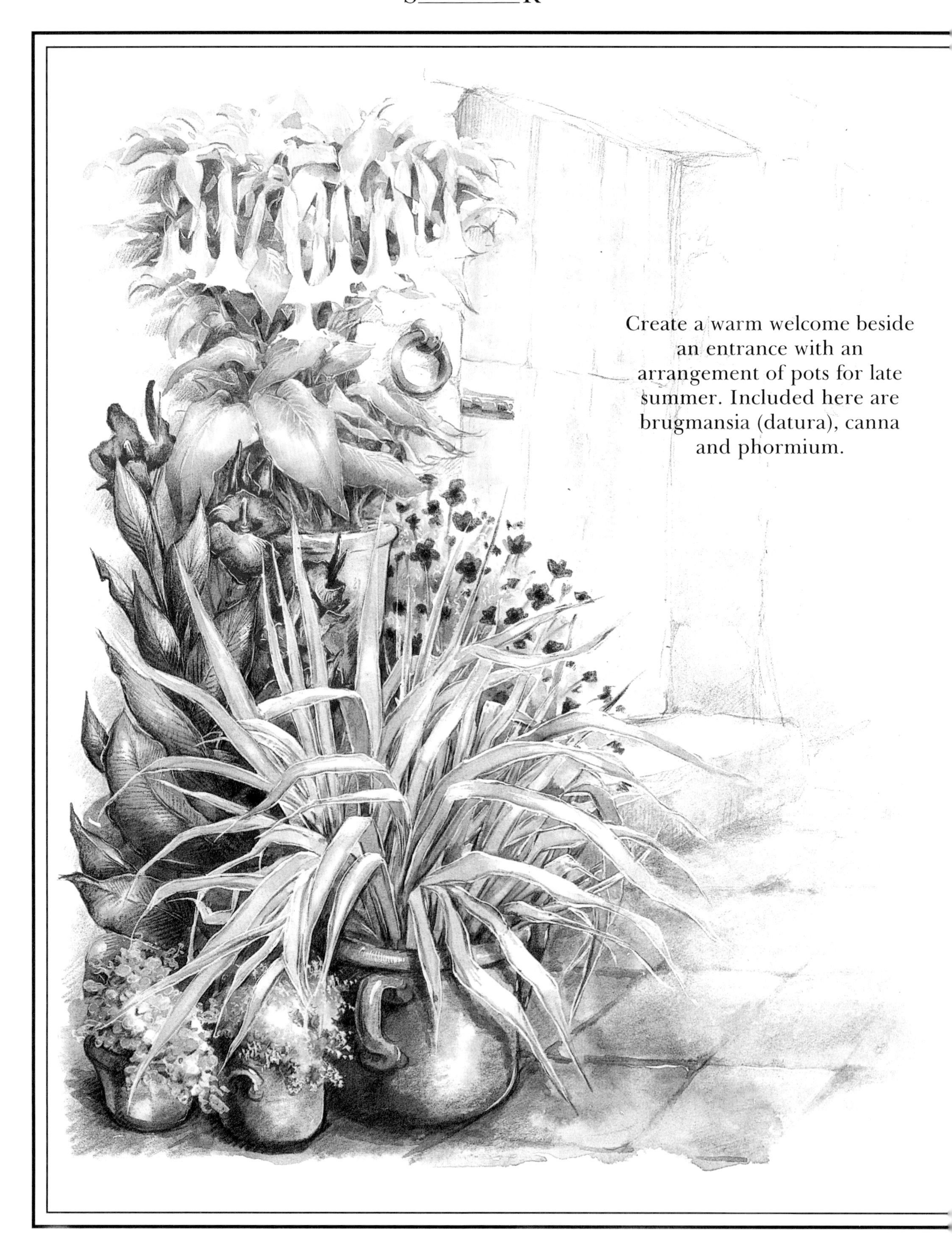

Create a warm welcome beside an entrance with an arrangement of pots for late summer. Included here are brugmansia (datura), canna and phormium.

SEPTEMBER

ALTHOUGH September sees the beginning of autumn, more often than not the days remain pleasantly warm and are, in reality, an extension of summer.

Japanese anemones, one of the treats of the later part of the year, are in full flower now and are accompanied by late pokers, rudbeckias and the first of the main show of asters.

Attention to detail will keep the garden fresh and interesting in the weeks ahead. Continued dead heading, the cutting back of summer perennials which have finished flowering and a light forking through the borders are all on-going tasks. Do not neglect the kitchen garden. As crops are harvested, clear away and compost debris to leave beds neat and tidy.

This late September border draws on *Verbena bonariensis*, asters and the purple cone flower, *Echinacea purpurea*, for autumn colour. In the background, glimpsed through the verbena, is the yellow daisy, *Rudbeckia fulgida* 'Goldsturm'.

◆ *Leave the heads of the verbena over winter to set seed. During frosty weather they will look particularly striking.*

All of the Japanese anemones will add grace and charm to end of season borders. Shown here is the pink *Anemone hupehensis* 'September Charm'. Other cultivars include purplish pink *A.h.* 'Hadspen Abundance', white *A.* × *hybrida* 'Honorine Jobert' and the mid-pink *A.* × *h.* 'Königin Charlotte'. Most grow in ordinary garden soil to around 1.5m/5ft.

Aconitum carmichaelii A rich blue, tall-growing perennial. It has poisonous, tuberous roots and will tolerate some shade. 1.5m × 30cm/5 × 1ft

Kniphofia caulescens Dramatic torch-like flowers rise above strappy leaves, deeply serrated, of grey-green. ❍, 1m × 60cm/ 3 × 2ft

Schizostylis coccinea Kaffir lilies thrive best in a damp situation. Plant where their nodding flower heads will be reflected in water. 60 × 30cm/2 × 1ft

***Aster thompsonii* 'Nanus'** The flowering period of this small, lilac aster extends from midsummer well into autumn. Use to wrap around taller growing perennials where its soft colour will harmonize with pinks, purples and silvers. 45 × 25cm/1½ft × 10in

***Aster novi-belgii* 'Lilac Time'** and ***Aster novi-belgii* 'Jenny'** Normally these Michaelmas daisies will be unlikely to start flowering until the end of the month. Massed together, as here, they make a bold statement.

◆ *Asters harmonize together well. There are seldom clashes of colour.*

Kirengeshoma palmata Lovely waxy lemon blooms. For successful cultivation, plant in semi-shade in humus-rich soil which is moisture retentive. ◐, 1m × 75cm/3 × 2½ft

◆ *During the flowering period do not allow to dry out. Water on a daily basis if necessary.*

Aster luteus Tiny, pale canary-yellow daisies cover this pretty aster during the autumn. The airy flowers are useful for cutting. 60 × 30cm/2 × 1ft

***Arctotis* × *hybrida* 'Apricot'** A tender South African plant in shades of red, white and yellow. Introduce into borders for a splash of late colour. ❍, 45 × 30cm/1½ × 1ft

Helianthus Young children will delight in growing traditional sunflowers from seed. Competitions may be held to grow the tallest. ❍, 2.1 × 1m/ 7 × 3ft

Senecio tanguticus Eye-catching perennial for the back of the border which, later on, will produce fluffy seed heads. 1.5m × 60cm/5 × 2ft

Gypsophila Fill gaps in the border with frothy pink or white flowered gypsophila. Best on free-draining soil. 1.2 × 1.2m/ 4 × 4ft

***Rudbeckia fulgida* 'Goldsturm'** A wonderful autumn perennial. Black-eyed daisies will flower right through autumn and even into winter if the weather is kind. Plant in blocks for maximum impact. ❍, 75 × 45cm/2½ × 1½ft

◆ *'Goldsturm' requires no staking. Plants may be increased by division every three or four years.*

SHRUBS AND TREES

The approach of autumn brings with it a second flowering, albeit intermittently, of a number of the shrubs whose main flowering period is much earlier in the year. It is rather like renewing old friendships. Of these many of the roses may be relied upon to provide a second flush of bloom, often going on right into winter. Late clematis prolong the season and may be employed to enliven trees and shrubs which no longer command centre stage. All of these are easy to cultivate and are pruned hard to the ground in the spring.

***Rosa moyesii* 'Geranium'** Early flowers of blood-red are followed by these startling heps which decorate the long, arching stems in autumn. 2.4 × 2.2m/8 × 7ft

◆ *Give this rose plenty of space to develop its natural, pleasing shape.*

Leycesteria formosa Distinctive, beetroot-coloured bracts enclose the tiny flowers of this shrub for late summer and early autumn. Shapely olive-green stems are hollow and should be reduced to ground level in spring. 2 × 2m/ 6 × 6ft

Clerodendrum bungei Flowers of magenta-pink are borne on fresh stems thrown up each spring from a wandering root-stock. 1.2m × 30cm/4 × 1ft

Buddleja crispa One of the most desirable of all buddlejas producing a succession of delicate lilac flowers from late summer. ❍, E, 1 × 1m/3 × 3ft

◆ *Plant in a very sheltered spot as this buddleja is particularly susceptible to cold.*

An early autumn planting which achieves impact through a close relationship of foliage and flower. Central to the scheme is a bold clump of *Heuchera* 'Rachel' whose dark leaves contrast with the prettily shaped, grey-green leaves of *Geranium renardii*.

Against a background of a dark holly, *Fuchsia magellanica* 'Gracilis Variegata' is a mass of flower.

Not everyone is, of course, in possession of a fine stone balustrade. But that is no reason for not growing these two splendid clematis which, flowering at the same time from July until September, are ideal companions. The pearly-white flowers of *Clematis* 'Huldine' show up well against the deep velvety blooms of *C. viticella* 'Royal Velours'. 'Huldine' will reach around 5m/16ft whilst 'Royal Velours' is slightly less vigorous at 3.5m/12ft. Other viticella hybrids of comparable size for a similar situation are 'Margot Koster' and 'Venosa Violacea'.

***Clematis* 'Rouge Cardinal'** Rich magenta flowers appear from June until the end of September, making this clematis worthy of inclusion in any garden. It prefers a sunny, south-facing position. Train against a wall, over a pergola or arch, through a shrub or grow in a container. 2.4–3m/8–10ft

***Clematis* × *eriostemon* 'Hendersonii'** An utterly charming clematis to stray through the border. Prune hard in the early part of the year. 2.4m/8ft

Clematis rehderiana Delightful, fragrant flowers need to be seen at eye level to appreciate fully their beauty. 2.4–3m/8–10ft

***Clematis* 'Lasurstern'** Flowers first in May and June and then again in August and September. The second flowering may be slightly less prolific. 3m/10ft

◆ *By planting 'Lasurstern' to grow against a north wall, flowers may effectively be delayed.*

Clematis tangutica Yellow lantern-like flowers typify this rampant species originating in China. Flowers, which continue well into autumn, are followed by lingering seed heads which later give a decorative quality to a winter landscape. 5m/16ft

***Hedera helix* 'Buttercup'** A magnificent golden-leafed form of ivy which should be grown in full sun to maintain the intense colour. Ivies are very suitable for most situations including ground cover. E, 2.7m/9ft

***Parthenocissus tricuspidata* 'Veitchii'** As September moves into October so the wonderful autumn foliage of the Boston ivy deepens to claret-red. This creeper is self-clinging by means of tiny tendrils. 20m/66ft

***Humulus lupulus* 'Aureus'** Yellow leaves of this sprawling form of hop will brighten up the dullest of days. Plant to grow up into a tree or train around a purpose-built support. 4m/13ft

◆ *Cut back to ground level at some point during the winter or early spring.*

TRANSPLANT EVERGREENS
The start of autumn is a good time in which to move evergreen trees and shrubs. In transplanting, remember to keep the roots out of the ground for as short a time as possible.

Prepare the planting hole to the correct size in advance and insert a stake to steady the new planting. Dig out the tree or shrub to be moved taking care as this is done not to damage any roots.

Insert into the new position and back fill with well rotted garden compost. Water well and continue to do so until rain.

ESTABLISH A NEW LAWN
Warm September rains make this month an ideal time in which to establish new lawns, either from seed or using turf. In both cases ground should be properly prepared and levelled to form a firm surface.

Seed should be sown evenly on a dry, windless day at a rate of 50g/2oz per square metre/yard. After sowing, soil should be given a very light raking partially to cover the seed. Germination should take place within ten days.

Before laying turves rake the surface of the ground to facilitate the grass roots binding into the earth. Place turves in such a manner that they will bond, like bricks in a wall, and sieve finely sifted soil into any gaps. Water and lightly roll until the lawn is durable.

PLANT BULBS FOR SPRING
Bulbs which have been offered for sale since August may be planted during this month. A head start made now will mean there is much less to do when the weather becomes colder and the ground less hospitable.

Begin with crocuses, daffodils, hyacinth, scillas and winter aconites. Tulips are better left until October or even November.

DIVIDE AND REPLANT IRISES
Where iris rhizomes have become overcrowded, resulting in fewer flowers, they should be divided. Normally this takes place after flowering. September is a suitable month in which to carry this out although the job could be put off until October.

Follow the method outlined on page 100. See that the soil where replanting is to take place is replenished. This may be done by forking in well rotted compost or manure.

SOW ANNUALS FOR SPRING
Very hardy annuals sown now, as opposed to those sown in the spring, will bloom much earlier on in the new season.

Sown in trays, and then transplanted and potted on, they may be kept over winter in a cold greenhouse or frame before setting out in position when the worst of the weather is over.

CHECK LIST

- Continue general garden maintenance (p.187).
- Plant late-flowering clematis for seasonal colour (pp.194–5, 196).
- Establish a new lawn (p.198).
- Transplant evergreens (p.198).
- Plant spring bulbs (p.198).
- Divide irises (p.199).
- Sow hardy annuals for spring (p.199).
- Move pots of tender plants, like pelargoniums (also known as geraniums) and fuchsias, indoors before first frosts (p.211).

AUTUMN PLANTING
Containerized plants, available throughout the year, have resulted in a move away from traditional autumn planting. However, warm soil, more certain rainfall and workable ground make this an excellent season for planting perennials and biennials. Young plants set out now will have plenty of time to establish and put on new growth before the close of year.

OCTOBER

OCTOBER, and autumn closes in on the garden. But it does so in a blaze of glory. Michaelmas daisies are at their most spectacular, a mixture of strong and pastel hues contributing vibrancy and immediacy to late season borders. They are not alone. This is a month for autumn bulbs – colchicums, crocus and cyclamen all commence their flowering season.

Elsewhere events take an exciting turn. Leaves colour, berries are illuminated and the first frosts etch the garden in a sensational and often surprising manner.

Spend time this month on some routine chores. Lawns will benefit from scarification where they have become compacted and should, in any case, be given an autumn feed. Continue to cut grass, with the mower blades set high, as long as weather permits. Winter digging, where appropriate, may be started and any autumn pruning undertaken.

As this shows, the autumn garden need never be dull. Asters combine with late flowering perennials such as *Solidago* (golden rod) and sedums to produce an effective and colourful display. Note how the grass path is curved. This draws the eye on, suggesting something new and of interest just around the corner.

Reds and golds typify autumn so this strong combination of rudbeckia and physalis is totally in keeping with the season. *Physalis alkekengii*, or Chinese lantern, produces these ornamental and edible fruits from inconspicuous cream flowers. 45 × 60cm/1½ × 2ft

◆ *Physalis will thrive in almost any situation, increasing by running roots.*

This large stand of solidago contrasts well with a pale lilac Michaelmas daisy. Golden rod is inclined to be a spreading perennial and is unsuitable for inclusion in a small border. Short, compact varieties are available like *S. canadensis* 'Golden Baby' which grows to around 60cm/2ft.

Low-growing asters edge the path in this mixed border where the emphasis is firmly placed on providing a contrast of form and texture. Soft perennials serve to highlight the shapes of shrubs and evergreen trees. Most striking are the prominent clumps of yucca (extreme right), a shape reflected in the central phormium.

Nerine bowdenii Heralding from South Africa, these bulbs prefer a warm situation in free-draining soil. Hardy except in very exposed areas. ○, 45 × 20cm/ 1½ft × 8in

Autumn crocuses are suitable for an open, sunny position where they may be left to increase. Bulbs should be planted from August onwards to a depth of 5cm/2in.

Liriope muscari Liriope comes into its own through the autumn. Flowers are quite small and are often disguised by the leaves. 30 × 45cm/1 × 1½ft

Persicaria campanulata An easy, spreading perennial for the back of the border. Flower heads look good until blackened by frost.
1 × 1m/3 × 3ft

Colchicum speciosum Sturdy flowers of rosy-lilac look splendid either naturalized in grass or as an underplanting to shrubs. ❍,
20 × 20cm/8 × 8in

Cyclamen hederifolium A long-lived plant whose flowers appear just as the silvery-green, ivy-type leaves begin to unfurl.
10 × 20cm/4 × 8in

***Physostegia virginiana* 'Variegata'** Leaves are edged white which, combined with the dark lilac-pink tubular flowers, make this a showy late perennial.
30 × 30cm/1 × 1ft

◆ *Physostegia is known as the obedient plant. Flower stalks, when moved, stay in place.*

SHRUBS AND TREES

Brilliant orange, burnished gold, crimson and bronze. The turning leaves of autumn are one of the principal joys of the season. Illustrated are the upright-growing *Malus tschonoskii*, the aptly named bonfire tree, *Acer palmatum* 'Osakazuki' and *Amelanchier* 'Ballerina'. All these are set against a background of the soft yellow leaves of *Rosa rugosa* 'Alba'. Imagine the intensity of this foliage caught in the rays of a dying sun. Indeed, it is worth bearing this point in mind when planting trees and shrubs for their autumn colour.

Parthenocissus quinquefolia This is the true Virginia creeper which turns such an outstanding colour before the leaves fall. A rampant self-clinging climber. 12m/39ft

◆ *As an alternative to covering a building, grow this climber through an established tree where it will hang in festoons.*

Euonymus alatus Grow this bushy shrub for its conspicuous autumn colour. Dull green leaves of spring and summer change to a wonderful crimson. 3 × 3m/ 10 × 10ft

***Acer palmatum* 'Dissectum'** Finely cut leaves are truly burnished before they fall. This compact acer is an excellent choice for a small garden where, growing slowly in part shade, it will eventually reach 1.2 × 1.5m/ 4 × 5ft.

Acer palmatum atropurpureum (*right*) Purple foliage becomes bright red at this time of year. A small grove of this tree, where space permits, would be a splendid addition to a garden. 4.5 × 4.5m/15 × 15ft

***Cotinus coggygria* 'Royal Purple'** This shrub is commonly known as the smoke tree. These July flower plumes are followed by bright red, autumn foliage. 4 × 4m/13 × 13ft

Vitis coignetiae The crimson glory vine is shown here trained on a pillar. The leaves are slowly turning from green to deep wine-red. 15m/49ft

Liquidambar styraciflua Outstanding autumn colouring. These leaves of richest claret will remain on the tree well into winter. 16 × 8m/52 × 26ft

◆ *Unfortunately this is not a tree for a small garden.*

***Rhus glabra* 'Laciniata'** A very hardy, free-suckering shrub which is grown principally for its late colour. Because of its running habit it can become a bit of a nuisance so is best suited to informal areas. 3 × 3m/10 × 10ft

This cottage wall is positively aglow with the bright berries of a wall trained pyracantha. These evergreen shrubs are ideal for this purpose as they provide something of interest throughout all seasons. E, 2.1m/7ft

◆ *Named forms include 'Dart's Red', 'Mohave' and 'Orange Charmer'.*

***Vitis vinifera* 'Purpurea'** Blue-black grapes and leaves of deep purple. Grow vines for their ornamental quality. 7m/23ft

Callicarpa bodinieri var. ***geraldii*** Remarkable, lustrous berries possess a jewel-like quality. Foliage turns purple as the year progresses. 4 × 4m/13 × 13ft

Pernettya (syn. ***Gaultheria***) ***mucronata*** The colour of the fruits, white, pink, red, purple or black, depend on the clone. A shrub for acidic soil. ◐, E, 75cm × 1.2m/2½ × 4ft

Cornus kousa Every garden should, if possible, contain a specimen of this very elegant shrub. Summer flowers are followed by these fabulous, decorative strawberry-like fruits. 3.6 × 4m/12 × 13ft

◆ *Several forms of the Chinese dogwood are offered. 'Norman Hadden' is amongst the best named.*

***Malus* 'Everest'** After the pinky-white flowers of spring this dwarf tree is later weighed down with scarlet crab apples. 3.6 × 2.4m/ 12 × 8ft

Arbutus unedo Rather strangely the flowers and fruit of the Killarney strawberry tree appear together in the autumn. Prefers acid soil. E, 5 × 5m/16 × 16ft

Rosa rugosa One of the pleasures of this rose at this time of year is the formation of these bright red, tomato-like heps. ❍, 1.5 × 1.5m/ 5 × 5ft

***Cotoneaster frigidus* 'Cornubia'** Clusters of scarlet berries hang in profusion below semi-evergreen leaves on this large tree-like shrub. Most types of cotoneaster reward with either foliage effects or massed berries. 7 × 7m/23 × 23ft

◆ *Cotoneasters are hardy, quick to grow and easy to establish in most ordinary garden soils.*

PLANT NEW HEDGES

October represents a good month in which to establish new hedges.

Ground must be well prepared in advance, incorporating where possible plenteous amounts of organic matter.

These new box plants will respond to an application of bonemeal in the spring to speed growth.

Many types of hedging will be available bare-rooted at this time of year. Take advantage of cheaper prices.

PLANT BARE-ROOTED ROSES

Specialist rose growers, and some garden centres, offer bare-rooted roses for sale throughout the autumn. Buying in this way makes good sense, not least because they are often considerably cheaper than those which are container grown.

If, at the time of purchase, ground is unprepared or the weather too inclement for planting, then no harm will come if roses are 'heeled-in'. This involves no more than burying the roots in a trench of garden soil mixed with well rotted compost.

Before planting, prune roses to shape, cutting above an outward facing bud. Also trim roots to encourage new growth. Ensure that planting holes are well lined with generous quantities of compost and that roses are watered in.

PUTTING THE GARDEN TO BED
As the weeks of autumn pass, so the approach of winter focuses more in the mind. Start now to tackle some of the jobs which will help keep the garden in good shape during the months ahead.

Pots of tender plants need to be removed to a frost-free environment. Those which are to remain outside may need to be lagged as a precaution against damage or frost.

Cut down spent perennials, remove frosted annuals, lightly fork borders and apply a mulch if desired. Fallen leaves will start to pose problems in many cases. Sweep from lawns, remove from gulleys and clear from small plants.

CHECK LIST

- Scarify lawns and apply an autumn fertilizer (p.200).
- Start winter digging.
- Take account of autumn colour when choosing shrubs and trees (p.204).
- Plant bare-rooted roses (p.210).
- Establish new hedges (p.210).
- Begin preparations for winter (p.211).
- Plant tulips.

LIFT TENDER PERENNIALS
Tender perennials should now be lifted from the open ground before the worst of the weather sets in. For convenience they may be potted up and stored in a greenhouse which is kept frost-free over the winter. Dahlia tubers should be overwintered as described on page 184.

A colourful, interesting and carefully planned late autumn show. Seen against a background of dark leafed mahonia and golden variegated euonymus, the purple spikes of *Liriope platyphylla* are displayed to advantage.

NOVEMBER

EVER SHORTENING DAYS, wet and windy weather, trees shedding their leaves, all make their mark on November. Colour in the borders starts to fade. Increasingly interest depends on evergreen and variegated shrubs. Structure, in the form of bare trees, hedges and shapely plants begins to take over.

***Salix alba vitellina* 'Britzensis'**
Shed of their leaves, the stems of this shrubby willow glow scarlet and orange in the late sun. They will remain looking attractive until pollarded in March (see page 39).

Much thought has been given here to achieving year-round interest. Brilliant red stems of *Cornus alba* are a handsome backdrop to a late yucca, in full flower, which appears to erupt from a carpet of evergreen hebe.

Deep red, purple and white fruits of evergreen pernettya add sparkle to this artfully contrived composition. Rising from a sea of winter-flowering heather, already in bud, is a group of golden stemmed willow.

For sheer elegance at the year's end there is little to rival the glorious plumes of the pampas grass, *Cortaderia selloana*. This imaginative planting allows the white feathers to be reflected in the water. Annually the sharply edged leaves should be cut close to the ground (see page 38).

***Viburnum tinus* 'Eve Price'** Flowering from now onwards, notwithstanding the weather. Plant close to a path to appreciate the delicious fragrance. E, 2.4 × 2.4/8 × 8ft

***Viburnum* × *bodnantense* 'Dawn'** Another beautifully scented shrub. In flower throughout the winter but most blooms appear during milder periods. 3.5 × 3.5m/12 × 12ft

Choisya ternata An invaluable shrub as a specimen, hedge or in a mixed border. The Mexican orange blossom is hardy but dislikes intense cold. E, 2 × 2m/ 6 × 6ft

Fatsia japonica Fatsia has all the appearance of only being suitable for indoor cultivation. Its splendidly large leaves look exotic but are actually quite tough. Tolerates sun or shade. E, 3 × 3m/10 × 10ft

Mahonia lomariifolia Sadly this magnificent scented mahonia is not fully hardy. However, given the warmth and protection of a wall, as here, it should not prove to be a problem. E, 3 × 2m/10 × 6ft

Skimmia japonica Rich, seasonal berries come close to smothering this unfussy, evergreen shrub over the winter period. Grow skimmia to brighten up any dull or dark day. E, 60 × 60cm/2 × 2ft

◆ *To effect pollination, plant male and female varieties close together.*

***Euonymus fortunei* 'Emerald 'n' Gold'** The virtue of a shrub such as this one is that it has something to contribute all year. In summer it can be toned down with associated planting but during autumn and winter its brightness is warmly appreciated. E, 1 × 1.5m/3 × 5ft

◆ *For a silver-based scheme, plant* E. fortunei *'Emerald Gaiety'.*

***Elaeagnus pungens* 'Dicksonii'** An ideal shrub with which to brighten up a featureless border. As with all variegated shrubs care should be taken to cut out any branches where the leaves have reverted. ❍, E, 2.4 × 3m/8 × 10ft

***Hedera colchica* 'Sulphur Heart'** Long, rather drooping leaves are lifted with bold splashes of yellow on this evergreen climbing ivy. Ivies thrive in almost any situation and are very tolerant of atmospheric pollution. E, 4.5m/15ft

◆ *The number of named forms is huge.* H. helix *'Glacier', 'Goldheart' and 'Silver Queen' are among the best known.*

***Aucuba japonica* 'Gold Dust'** All the aucubas are valuable shrubs for difficult situations. The leaves of this particular form are speckled gold, hence the name. Red berries are produced from autumn to spring. E, 2.4 × 2.4m/ 8 × 8ft

Hollies, with their abundant berries, are seldom thought of as climbers. Many, in fact, are wholly suitable for training against walls or for clipping into a variety of shapes as another medium for topiary. *Ilex aquifolium* 'J.C. van Tol' is used here to clothe the wall of a house. This particular holly has virtually spineless leaves and produces a good crop of red berries.

***Cornus stolonifera* 'Flaviramea'** Grow this dogwood as much for its greenish-yellow stems as for the small white flowers produced in summer. 2 × 4m/6 × 12ft

***Lonicera nitida* 'Baggesen's Gold'** This small leafed shrub may be clipped into shape. In a sunny situation it retains the brilliance of its colour. ❍, E, 1.5 × 2m/5 × 6ft

***Thuja occidentalis* 'Rheingold'** Conifers come into their own during winter when their shapes become more pronounced in the absence of other distractions. E, 3 × 1.5m/10 × 5ft

◆ *Often sold as a miniature conifer, 'Rheingold' will eventually make a substantial tree.*

***Ligustrum ovalifolium* 'Aureum'** Golden privet is a useful, fast-growing shrub to plant as a screen or even to form a brightly coloured hedge. Semi-evergreen, it will lose its leaves if the winter is severe. 4 × 3m/13 × 10ft

***Vinca minor* 'Aureovariegata'** Use this lesser periwinkle where ground cover is required and where little else will grow. E, 15cm/6in (spread indefinite)

GARDEN WASTE
Leaves swept from lawns, raked from borders or simply cleared from paths and drives will make excellent leaf mould.

Simply gather together within an open wire-framed cage, firm down and leave. Within a year the leaves will have compressed to form a nutritious mould which may be used directly on the garden.

With the exception of woody stems, which should be chopped, shredded or burnt, all garden and household waste should be composted. Left to rot for eighteen months or so it will make an excellent medium with which to enrich the soil.

ATTEND TO GARDEN PONDS
Ponds require a certain amount of attention as autumn moves into winter.

Where possible, clear leaves and other end of season debris from the water. An accumulation of decaying matter will contribute to a build-up of toxic gases.

Cut down surrounding perennials and fork over the soil. Giant leaves of *Gunnera manicata* should be folded over the crown of the plant to provide protection from cold.

Submersible pumps may be removed, serviced and stored in preparation for next season.

Finally, fish will survive the winter months without feeding. Cease feeding until spring.

DIG AND MANURE VEGETABLE BEDS
Over winter prepare for spring by digging and manuring the kitchen garden. The addition of any organic matter will greatly improve soil structure.

TAKE HARDWOOD CUTTINGS
Many trees and shrubs, like this *Sambucus* (elder), are readily propagated from hardwood cuttings taken during November.

Select a cutting around 30cm/1ft in length. Make a clean, sloping cut at the top just above a leaf joint, another straight one at the bottom below a joint. Dip the lower part into a hormone rooting powder.

Dig a small trench in a shady spot and line the bottom with a mixture of sharp sand and peat. Rest the bottom of the labelled cutting on to this base. Infill with soil, firming in thoroughly to eliminate any air pockets.

Cuttings should root within twelve months. Once rooted they may either be potted up or planted out.

CHECK LIST

- Choose variegated and evergreen shrubs for year-round interest (pp.214–219).
- Clear ponds of autumn debris, service electrical pumps and stop feeding fish (p.220).
- Collect leaves for leaf mould (p.220).
- Manure vegetable beds (p.220).
- Take hardwood cuttings (p.221).
- Plant bare-rooted trees and shrubs (p.27).
- Complete the planting of tulips as soon as possible this month.

PLANT FRUIT TREES
Late autumn, while the soil may still be worked with relative ease, is the time to plant fruit trees. These may be bought either bare-rooted, as balled plants or in containers. Prepare ground beforehand and stake where necessary.

DECEMBER

WITH DECEMBER, and the approach of winter, the garden takes on an air of quietness. After the activity of summer and autumn, there is now an absence of urgency, a calm repose.

Cold but clear wintery days may be used to tackle those jobs which are forgotten during busier times. Trees and shrubs which overhang or obstruct paths may be pruned back to give ease of access. Ditches, gulleys and drains cleaned out and kept clear will prevent a build-up of surface water during periods of heavy rainfall. Apply wood preservative to garden seats and sheds and structures such as pergolas, archways and trellises.

Look carefully and critically at the hard landscaping and structure of the garden, noting how it may be improved in the coming year. Indeed, one of the delights of winter is to see the bare bones of the garden, liberated for a short while from the colour and frippery of summer.

Frosted heads of *Stipa gigantea*, a large clump-forming grass, make a dramatic impact seen against the woolly, grey-green foliage of *Ozothamnus rosmarinifolius*.

◆ *Stipa may be cut back to ground level in early spring (see page 38).*

***Miscanthus sinensis* 'Silver Feather'** Grasses such as this one are an excellent foil to other plantings. Their spectacular summer display is matched in winter with an extraordinary beauty. 2m × 60cm/ 6 × 2ft

Fargesia nitida Also known as *Sinarundinaria*, this small leafed bamboo is noted for its distinctive purplish stems. Older clumps tend to push themselves out of the ground so are best lifted and divided in May when this happens. E, 5m/15ft × indefinite spread

The approach to this cottage is sympathetically planted with a series of clipped yew cones. Not only do they complement the plain, flagged path but are deliberately kept to a size which does not become overwhelming. In winter, possibly in snow, their structure would be even more pronounced.

***Picea glauca* 'Albertiana'** Slow-growing conifers add important structure to rock gardens. They also suggest scale in such situations. E, 1m × 45cm/3 × 1½ft in ten years

Abies balsamea* f. *hudsonia A miniature, slow-growing form of the Balsam fir with aromatic foliage. This conifer is tolerant of chalky conditions. E, 1 × 1m/ 3 × 3ft

***Juniperus communis* 'Compressa'** A tiny evergreen tree which is small enough to be included in a container garden. Position out of cold winds. E, 75 × 15cm/ 2½ft × 6in

***Juniperus horizontalis* 'Wiltonii'** Permanent ground cover is achieved by planting this low, spreading juniper of steely-blue. The ultimate spread is likely to be around 4m/13ft.

◆ *In the main, conifers may be relied upon for hardiness and long life expectancy.*

***Hebe* 'Boughton Dome'** Grow this dense, rounded hebe for its year-round interest. Fine foliage makes up for the few flowers. E, 75 × 75cm/2½ ×2½ft

***Brachyglottis* 'Sunshine'** Previously known as *Senecio greyi*, the evergreen grey foliage is particularly valuable in winter. ○, E, 1.2 × 2m/4 × 6ft

Pittosporum tenuifolium One of the best species of these highly ornamental, evergreen shrubs. Hardiness cannot be relied upon so grow in a sheltered situation. E, 5 × 4m/16 × 13ft

Beautifully grown box spirals flank the approach to this flight of steps. A small leafed ivy softens the elegant, basket-weave containers whilst a newly planted hedge of box extends the formality.

Jasminum nudiflorum Winter jasmine is much loved and, accordingly, widely grown. Here it has been trained to smother a wall with its splendid yellow blossom and green, whippy stems. 3m/10ft

◆ *Around a doorway, along a boundary fence or cascading down a bank, this jasmine is totally deserving of its popularity.*

Iris foetidissima When the seed pods of the Gladwin iris burst open in winter, these vibrant orange seeds are revealed. E, 45 × 60cm/1½ × 2ft

Arum italicum Winter sees the emergence of these wonderfully marked leaves which have remained dormant throughout the summer. ●, 25 × 20cm/ 10 × 8in

Euphorbia myrsinites Heavy with frost, the sprawling stems of this ground-hugging euphorbia strike a very chilling note. ❍, E, 15 × 60cm/6in × 2ft

Garrya elliptica Favour this handsome shrub with a warm wall to afford it protection from the worst of the frosts. Long-lasting male catkins may open as early as November or, depending on the weather, be delayed until February. E, 4 × 3m/13 × 10ft

◆ *Even longer, more graceful catkins are produced on the form 'James Roof'.*

COLD WEATHER PRECAUTIONS
A little time spent affording some of the plants in the garden protection from the worst of the weather will pay dividends.

Unwanted conifer branches are used here to blanket a tender climber which is growing against this wall. In most cases this will be enough to ensure a plant's survival. Perennials of doubtful hardiness will usually come through if the crown is covered either with a mulch of compost or old fern leaves weighted down. Garden fleece is useful for protecting tender plants.

If heavy snow falls, try to spare some moments to brush or shake it off trees and shrubs where its weight may cause branches to snap. Hedges, too, will be better without a capping of snow.

Wind will also be a problem. Check ties and stakes on all vulnerable shrubs. Cut back a third of each stem of tree mallows (*Lavatera*) to prevent wind rock. If you prune roses in autumn instead of spring (see page 38) you will lessen the danger of wind rock, but new shoots might suffer frost damage.

Refirm plants that have been lifted by severe frost.

Protect newly planted shrubs with rabbit-guards or netting if rabbits are a problem in your garden.

Outside water taps should be switched off at the main and then left open. To be effective, lagging should itself be waterproof.

Although not always inevitable, plant losses do and will occur. Treat these philosophically – they are part of the spirit of gardening.

CARING FOR WILDLIFE
In the depths of winter, give some thought to wildlife coping with cold and food shortages.

At times when the temperature consistently remains below freezing, melt a small area of ice on the pond to release trapped gases that could be harmful to fish. This may be gently done by holding a container of boiling water on the surface.

Birds will be grateful for any scraps put out for them. Do this on a regular basis and they will reward by returning to the feeding spot day after day. Ensure a plentiful supply of fresh water.

CHECK LIST

- Prune overhanging trees and shrubs (p.222).
- Clean out ditches and drains (p.222).
- Apply preservative to exposed wood (p.222).
- Give tender plants some form of protection (p.228).
- Dislodge snow from trees and shrubs (p.228).
- Protect plants from wind (p.228).
- Switch off outside water (p.228).
- Care for wildlife (p.229).

STORE TERRACOTTA POTS
Terracotta pots are not necessarily totally frost resistant. Hessian or bubble wrap secured around terracotta pots, too large or heavy to move under cover, will prevent the clay from splintering.

Anemone blanda 'White Splendour'

CALENDAR

The following are chronological flowering lists, though in some cases shrubs have been included for their interesting foliage or fruits. The precise month of flowering will often vary according to weather and location; for this reason the season has been given after each month and it may be helpful to use this when planning planting schemes. Flowering periods will in any case overlap calendar months and many plants will remain in flower for several weeks or even months.

Numbers in brackets refer to pages where plants are described.

January–February (Early Year)

Chionodoxa (Glory of the snow) (17)
Crocus (14, 17)
Cyclamen coum (15)
Eranthis (Winter aconite) (16)
Galanthus (Snowdrop) (16)
Hellebores (16)
Hepatica
Iris danfordiae
I. histrioides
I. reticulata (17)
I. unguicularis (Algerian iris) (14)
Narcissus bulbocodium (Hoop-petticoat daffodil) (17)

Lysichiton americanus

N. cyclamineus
Pulmonaria (Lungwort) (34)
Scilla mischtschenkoana

Shrubs and Trees
Abeliophyllum distichum
Chimonathus praecox (Wintersweet) (22)
Clematis cirrhosa (22)
Cornus mas
Daphne odora (23)
Erica carnea (Heather) (23)
E. darleyensis
Garrya elliptica (Tassel bush) (227)
Hamamelis (Witch hazel) (21)
Jasminum nudiflorum (Winter jasmine) (226)
Lonicera fragrantissima (23)
Prunus × subhirtella 'Autumnalis'
Sarcococca (Sweet box) (21)
Viburnum tinus (214)

March (Early Spring)

Anemone appenina (33)
A. blanda
Bergenia (34)
Corydalis (32)
Crocus (17)
Darmera peltata (Umbrella plant)
Doronicum (Leopard's bane) (46)
Epimedium (Barrenwort) (32)
Erythronium dens-canis (Dog's-tooth violet) (35)
Hellebore (34)
Iberis
Ipheion (33)
Lysichiton americanus (Yellow skunk cabbage)
Muscari (Grape hyacinth) (29)
Narcissus hybrids (Daffodils) (29)
Omphalodes cappadocica

Darmera peltata

Primula (Primrose, Polyanthus) (31, 32, 44, 45)
Pulmonaria (Lungwort) (34)
Ranunculus (Buttercup) (34)
Scilla (31)
Symphytum grandiflorum (Comfrey)
Tulipa greigii
T. kaufmanniana (28)
Viola odorata (Sweet violet)

Shrubs & Trees
Camellia (36)
Corylopsis pauciflora
Daphne mezereum
D. blagayana
Erica arborea (Tree heath)
Forsythia (36)
Mahonia aquifolium
Parrotia
Pieris (23)
Prunus dulcis (Ornamental almond)
P. mume (Japanese apricot)
P. × *yedoensis* (Yoshino cherry)
Rhododendron 'Praecox' (36)
Sycopsis sinensis
Viburnum × *burkwoodii* (36)

April (Spring)

Alyssum saxatile (50)
Anemone nemorosa (51)
Arabis (48)
Arum (Cuckoo pint) (45)
Aubrieta (49)
Bellis (Daisy) (66)
Brunnera (46)
Caltha palustris (Marsh marigold) (47)
Cheiranthus (Wallflower) (41)
Cortusa matthioli
Dicentra (47, 51)

Dodecatheon meadia

Dodecatheon meadia
Doronicum (Leopard's bane) (46)
Euphorbia (Spurge) (50)
Fritillaria (Fritillary) (42, 43)
Hyacinth (40)
Lamium (Deadnettle) (44)
Leucojum vernum (Spring snowflake) (42)
Lunaria (Honesty) (64, 65)
Lysichiton camschatcensis (Skunk cabbage) (47)
Muscari (Grape hyacinth)
Narcissus (Daffodil) (42)
Ornithogalum nutans (Star of Bethlehem)
Oxalis acetosella (Wood sorrel)
Polygonatum (Solomon's seal)
Primula (44, 45)
Pulsatilla vulgaris (Pasque flower) (49)
Sanguinaria canadensis (50)
Saxifrage (51)
Silene dioica (Red campion)
Symphytum grandiflorum (Comfrey)
Tulips, early hybrids (41, 48)
Uvularia grandiflora (Bellwort) (46)
Veronica 'Georgia Blue' (45)
Vinca (Periwinkle)
Viola (Pansy)

Shrubs & Trees
Acer pseudoplatanus 'Brilliantissimum' (53)
Amelanchier
Berberis (Barberry) (56)
Camellia (54)
Ceanothus impressus
Chaenomeles (53)
Choisya (79)
Clematis (57)
Coronilla glauca
Cytisus (79)
Daphne × burkwoodii
Fothergilla

Geranium malviflorum

Kerria
Magnolia (54)
Malus (Crab apple) (56)
Osmanthus (56)
Prunus (Japanese cherry tree) (55)
Pyrus salicifolia 'Pendula'
Rhododendron hybrids (55)
Ribes (Currant)
Salix (Willow) (52, 56)
Skimmia (56)
Spiraea 'Arguta' (Bridal wreath) (79)
Viburnum × *burkwoodii*
V. × *juddii* (55)

May (Late Spring/Early Summer)

Ajuga (Bugle)
Allium aflatunense (74)
Anthemis punctata (Chamomile)
Aquilegia (Columbine) (62)
Arisaema
Armeria (Thrift) (64)
Asphodeline lutea (110)
Camassia (75)
Cardamine pratensis (Lady's smock)
Celmisia
Centaurea (66)
Convallaria (Lily-of-the-valley) (75)
Dicentra (69)
Disporum sessile
Erinus alpinus (Fairy foxglove)
Erodium
Euphorbia (Spurge) (65)
Gentiana acaulis (67)
Geranium (Cranesbill) e.g. *G. malviflorum*
Geum rivale (70)
Helianthemum (103, 104)
Hesperis (Sweet rocket) (69)
Hyacinthoides non-scriptus (Bluebell) (74)
Incarvillea delavayi

Rheum palmatum

Iris, Californian hybrids (71)
Jeffersonia diphylla
Lavandula stoechas (Lavender) (122)
Leucojum aestivum (Summer snowflake)
Libertia (67)
Limnanthes (Poached egg flower) (70)
Linum
Lithodora diffusa
Lunaria (Honesty) (64, 65)
Meconopsis cambrica (Welsh poppy) (64)
Mertensia (70)
Myosotis (Forget-me-not) (64, 73)
Narcissus 'Hawera'
  N. poeticus var. *recurvus* (Pheasant's eye)
Orontium aquaticum (89)
Paeonia arietina (71)
  P. mlokosewitschii
  P. tenuifolia
Parochetus communis
Penstemon ('rock garden' forms)
Persicaria bistorta (Bistort)
Phlox (64)
Polemonium (107)
Primula sieboldii (68)
Rheum palmatum
Rhodohypoxis (74)
Smilacina (68)
Tellima grandiflora
Thalictrum (62)
Thermopsis (70)
Tiarella cordifolia (Foamflower)
Tolmiea menziesii
Trillium (68)
Trollius
Tulips (72, 73)
Vancouveria hexandra
Veronica gentianoides (67)
Viola (64, 67)

Daphne × burkwoodii

SHRUBS & TREES

Abutilon (125, 129)
Aesculus (76)
Akebia quinata (Chocolate vine)
Andromeda
Azaleas (84, 85)
Berberis thunbergii
Ceanothus (82)
Cercis (Judas tree) (78)
Choisya ternata (79)
Clematis montana (81) and early large flowered clematis
Convolvulus cneorum (83)
Crataegus (Hawthorn)
Crinodendron hookeranum
Cytisus (79)
Daphne × burkwoodii
D. tangutica
Drimys winteri
Eccremocarpus scaber (Chilean glory vine)
Embothrium coccineum
Exochorda (79)
Fothergilla (87)
Fremontodendron (87)
Genista (Broom) (87)
Halesia (Snowdrop tree) (83)
Hebe pinguifolia
Laburnum (87)
Leptospermum
Leucothoë
Lithodora
Magnolia liliiflora
Malus (Crab apple) (76)
Paeonia delavayi (Tree peony) (83)
P. suffruticosa (Tree peony) (83)
Paulownia
Pernettya
Philadelphus coronarius (Mock orange) (125)
Piptanthus
Potentilla (145)

Viburnum plicatum 'Mariesii'

Prunus – Japanese cherries (78)
Rhododendron (84, 85)
Rosa banksiae and early yellow roses (86)
R. moyesii (86)
R. rugosa (86)
Rubus tridel
Solanum crispum (121)
Sorbus aria (Whitebeam) (77)
Spiraea (79)
Syringa (Lilac) (80)
Tamarix gallica (Tamarisk)
Viburnum davidii
V. opulus (Guelder rose)
V. plicatum 'Mariesii'
Weigela (80)
Wisteria (88)

June (Early Summer/Midsummer)

Aethionema
Alchemilla (101)
Allium christophii
A. moly
Alstroemeria (136)
Anchusa
Anthericum
Aruncus
Asarina procumbens
Asphodeline (Asphodel) (110)
Asphodelus (Asphodel) (106)
Astrantia (Masterwort)
Baptisia (106)
Campanula (Bellflower) e.g. *C. latiloba*
Centaurea macrocephala (110)
Centranthus (Valerian) (103)
Cephalaria (110)
Corydalis lutea (102)
Crambe cordifolia (109)
Dactylorrizha (Orchid)
Delphinium (111)

Dictamnus albus 'Purpureus'

Dianthus (Pink) (102)
Dictamnus (Burning bush)
Digitalis (Foxglove) (99)
Eremurus (Foxtail lily) (108)
Erigeron (Fleabane)
Geranium (Cranesbill) e.g. *G. endressii* (98)
Geum (70)
Gillenia (108)
Gladiolus byzantinus (99)
Helianthemum (104)
Hemerocallis (63, 149, 166)
Heuchera (193)
Hosta (111)
Iris (100, 107)
Kniphofia (Red-hot poker) e.g. *K. 'Atlanta'*
Lathyrus grandiflorus (Everlasting pea)
Lilium martagon (Martagon lily) (108)
Linum
Lupinus arboreus (Tree lupin) (128)
L. polyphyllus (Lupin) (101)
Lychnis (74, 105)
Lysimachia punctata (137)
Mitella breweri
Nepeta (Catmint) (99)
Nicotiana (152)
Nigella damascena (Love-in-a-mist)
Nuphar lutea (Yellow water lily)
Nymphaea (Water lily)
Osteospermum (136)
Paeonia (Peony) (104)
Papaver orientale (Oriental poppy) (104)
Penstemon (104)
Phuopsis stylosa
Polemonium (107)
Primula vialii (167)
Ruta graveolens (Rue)
Salvia (107)
Scabiosa (Scabious) (100)
Sisyrinchium striatum
Stachys macrantha (106)

Erigeron karvinskianus

Stipa (222)
Thalictrum aquilegifolium (62)
Thermopsis (70)
Verbascum
Veronica 'Shirley Blue' (142)
Viola cornuta (108, 109)

Shrubs & Trees
Abutilon (125, 129)
Brachyglottis (syn. *Senecio*) (128)
Buddleja alternifolia (129)
B. globosa (128)
Bupleurum
Carpenteria (129)
Cistus, e.g. × *hybridus* (122)
Clematis, mid-season large-flowered, e.g. 'Mrs. Cholmondeley' (129)
Colutea arborescens
Cornus canadensis
C. kousa (124)
C. nuttallii
Davidia
Deutzia (127)
Embothrium
Enkianthus
Fabiana
Fremontodendron (87)
× *Halimiocistus* (122)
Hebe macrantha
Hydrangea anomala subsp. *petiolare* (124)
Kalmia (Calico bush) (128)
Kolkwitzia (Beauty bush) (129)
Laburnum (87)
Lavandula (Lavender) (122)
Lavatera 'Barnsley' (127)
Lonicera (Honeysuckle) (127)
Magnolia, e.g. M. × *watsonii*
Neillia (126)
Philadelphus (Mock orange), e.g. 'Belle Etoile' (125)

Cardiocrinum giganteum

Phlomis (128)
Potentilla fruticosa (145)
Rhododendron hybrids and late-flowering Azalea species
Roses, Old French, many shrub roses, climbers and ramblers
Schizandra
Solanum crispum (121)
Styrax

July (Midsummer)

Abutilon megapotamicum (144)
Acanthus (175)
Achillea (Yarrow) (147)
Agapanthus (140)
Agastache
Alstroemeria (136)
Amsonia (Blue star)
Anthemis tinctoria (137)
Arisaema
Aster × frikartii 'Mönch' (137)
Astilbe (164, 165)
Bedding Plants
Many of these annuals and tender subjects will be in flower until the first frosts:
Ageratum (152)
Alyssum
Antirrhinum (153)
Argyranthemum (Marguerite) (154)
Begonia (93)
Calendula (Marigold) (174)
Chrysanthemum parthenium (153)
Iberis (Candytuft)
Impatiens (Busy Lizzie) (153)
Lantana
Lobelia (160, 161)
Nemesia
Nicotiana (152)
Pansy (161)

Origanum laevigatum

Pelargonium (160)
Petunia (174)
Salvia splendens (153)
Tagetes (Marigold) (96, 174)
Verbena
Calamintha
Campanula (Bellflower) e.g. *C. alliariifolia* (141)
Canna (146)
Cardiocrinum
Catananche
Cimicifuga racemosa
Codonopsis
Convolvulus sabatius (137)
Coreopsis verticillata
Delphinium (143)
Dictamnus
Epilobium (Bay willow herb) (135)
Erigeron
Eryngium (137, 141)
Eupatorium
Filipendula (Meadowsweet) (167)
Gillenia (108)
Gypsophila (190)
Helichrysum italicum (149)
Hemerocallis hybrids (166)
Hosta (111)
Hyssopus officinalis (Hyssop)
Iris, e.g. *I. laevigata*
Kniphofia (Red-hot poker), e.g. *K.* 'Little Maid' (149)
Lathyrus latifolius (Everlasting pea) (142)
Liatris spicata (172)
Ligularia przewalskii (166)
Lilium (Lily), e.g. *L. regale* (163)
Lysimachia punctata (137)
Lythrum salicaria (Purple loosestrife)
Malva moschata
Monarda (136)
Nepeta (Catmint) (99)

Tradescantia 'Purple Dome'

Oenothera (149)
Origanum
Osteospermum (136)
Penstemon e.g. *P.* 'Apple Blossom' (136)
Persicaria affinis (167)
Phlox (140)
Primula florindae (166)
 P. vialii (167)
Rodgersia (167)
Romneya
Salvia patens (142)
Sanguisorba
Selinum tenuifolium
Sidalcea
Stachys olympica
Strobilanthes
Tradescantia
Tropaeolum (145)
 T. majus (Nasturtium) (146)
Veratrum
Verbena bonariensis (135)
Veronica austriaca 'Shirley Blue' (142)
Zantedeschia aethiopica (166)

Shrubs & Trees
Abelia
Buddleja globosa (128)
Callistemon rigidus (Bottlebrush) (145)
Calluna vulgaris
Catalpa
Ceratostigma
Clematis × *durandii* (149)
 C. viticella varieties (183, 195)
Cytisus battandieri (Morrocan broom) (159)
Escallonia (159)
Fuchsia (154)
Genista aetnensis (Mount Etna broom) (159)
Hebe hybrids (158)
Hoheria
Hydrangea arborescens

Passiflora 'Constance Elliot'

Hypericum calycinum (Rose of Sharon) (145)
Indigofera (158)
Lavandula (Lavender) (158)
Lavatera maritima (158)
Lonicera (Honeysuckle), e.g. *L. tragophylla* (151)
Maackia amurensis
Melianthus major (Honeybush)
Passiflora (Passion flower)
Phygelius
Potentilla (145)
Rosa – Floribunda (Cluster-flowered) varieties
R. filipes (156)
Hybrid Tea varieties
Santolina (Cotton lavender)
Solanum jasminoides (142)
Sorbaria (159)
Spartium
Spiraea

August (Late Summer)

Adenophora (Gland bellflower)
Alcea rosea (Hollyhock) (171)
Anemone hupehensis (Japanese anemone) (188)
A. × *hybrida* (Japanese anemone) (188)
Aster thompsonii 'Nanus' (189)
Buphthalmum
Canna (146)
Clematis heracleifolia (175)
Crinum
Crocosmia (171)
Curtonus
Echinacea (187)
Echinops (175)
Gentiana asclepiadea
Helenium (171)
Helianthus (171, 190)
Knautia

Fuchsia 'Lena' and *Clematis jackmanii* 'Superba'

Kniphofia, e.g. *K.* 'Cobra'
Lilium, e.g. Oriental lilies
Limonium
Lobelia cardinalis (172)
Macleaya
Sedum 'Ruby Glow' (175)
Senecio tanguticus (190)
Tritonia

Shrubs & Trees

Aralia elata (181)
Buddleja davidii (182)
Campsis
Caryopteris (180)
Ceanothus × *delileanus* 'Gloire de Versailles' (181)
Clematis viticella and late large-flowered forms (183)
Dorycnium
Escallonia 'Iveyi' (159)
Eucryphia (178)
Eupatorium
Fuchsia (172)
Hibiscus (181)
Hydrangeas (179)
Itea (180)
Koelreuteria (178)
Magnolia grandiflora (181)
Perovskia (180)
Polygonum baldschuanicum (183)
Potentilla fruticosa (145)
Schizophragma (183)
Tamarix ramosissima (Tamarisk) (176)
Yucca gloriosa (180)

September (Early Autumn)

Aconitum carmichaelii (189)
Arctotis (190)
Asters (Michaelmas daisies) (189)

Dendranthema 'Julia'

Dendranthema (171)
Echinacea (Coneflower) (187)
Gypsophila (190)
Helianthus (Sunflower) (171, 190)
Kirengeshoma (190)
Kniphofia (189)
Lobelia (172)
Miscanthus (223)
Rudbeckia (191)
Schizostylis (Kaffir lily) (189)
Sedum (175)

Shrubs & Trees
Buddleja crispa (193)
Clematis tangutica and late-flowering species (195–6)
Clerodendrum (193)
Leycesteria (192)
Parthenocissus (leaf colour) (197, 205)

October (Autumn)

Autumn crocus (202)
Colchicum (203)
Cyclamen hederifolium (203)
Liriope (202)
Nerine (202)
Persicaria (203)
Physalis (Chinese lantern) (201)
Physostegia (203)
Solidago (Golden rod) (201)
Tricyrtis (Toad lily)

Shrubs & Trees
Arbutus unedo (Strawberry tree)
Autumn fruits
- *Callicarpa* (208)
- *Cornus* (Dogwood) 208
- *Cotoneaster* (209)
- *Malus* (Crab apple) (209)

Pyracantha

Pernettya (208)
Pyracantha (Firethorn) (207)
Roses (209)
Viburnum opulus (Guelder rose)
Autumn leaf colour
Acer (Maple) (205)
Amelanchier (204)
Cotinus (Smoke bush) (206)
Euonymus (205)
Liquidamber (207)
Parthenocissus (197, 205)
Rhus (Sumach) (206)
Vitis (Vine) (206, 208)

November (Late Autumn)

SHRUBS & TREES
Aucuba (217)
Choisya ternata (214)
Fatsia (214)
Hippophae rhamnoides
Mahonia lomariifolia (214)
Skimmia (215)
Viburnum × *bodnantense* (214)
V. tinus (214)

December (Early Winter)

Iris unguicularis (Algerian iris) (14)

SHRUBS & TREES
Garrya elliptica (Tassel bush) (227)
Jasminum nudiflorum (Winter jasmine) (226)

INDEX